Physical Characteristics of Komondor
(from the American Kennel Club breed standard)

Body: Characterized by a powerful, deep chest, which is muscular and proportionately wide. The breast is broad and well-muscled. The belly is somewhat drawn up at the rear. The rump is wide, muscular and slopes slightly towards the root of the tail.

Tail: A continuation of the rump line, hanging and long enough to reach the hocks. Slightly curved upwards and/or to one side at its end.

Hindquarters: The steely, strong bone structure is covered with highly developed muscles. The legs are straight as viewed from the rear. Stifles are well-bent. Rear dewclaws must be removed.

Color: White, but not always the pure white of a brushed coat. In the ideal specimen the skin is gray.

Coat: Characteristic of the breed is the dense, protective coat. A grown dog is entirely covered with a heavy coat of these tassel-like cords, which form naturally.

Size: Dogs 27.5 inches and up at the withers; bitches 25.5 inches and up at the withers. Dogs are approximately 100 pounds and up, bitches approximately 80 pounds and up at maturity, with plenty of bone and substance.

Feet: Strong, rather large and with close, well-arched toes. Pads are hard, elastic and black or gray. Ideally, nails are black or gray, although light nails are acceptable.

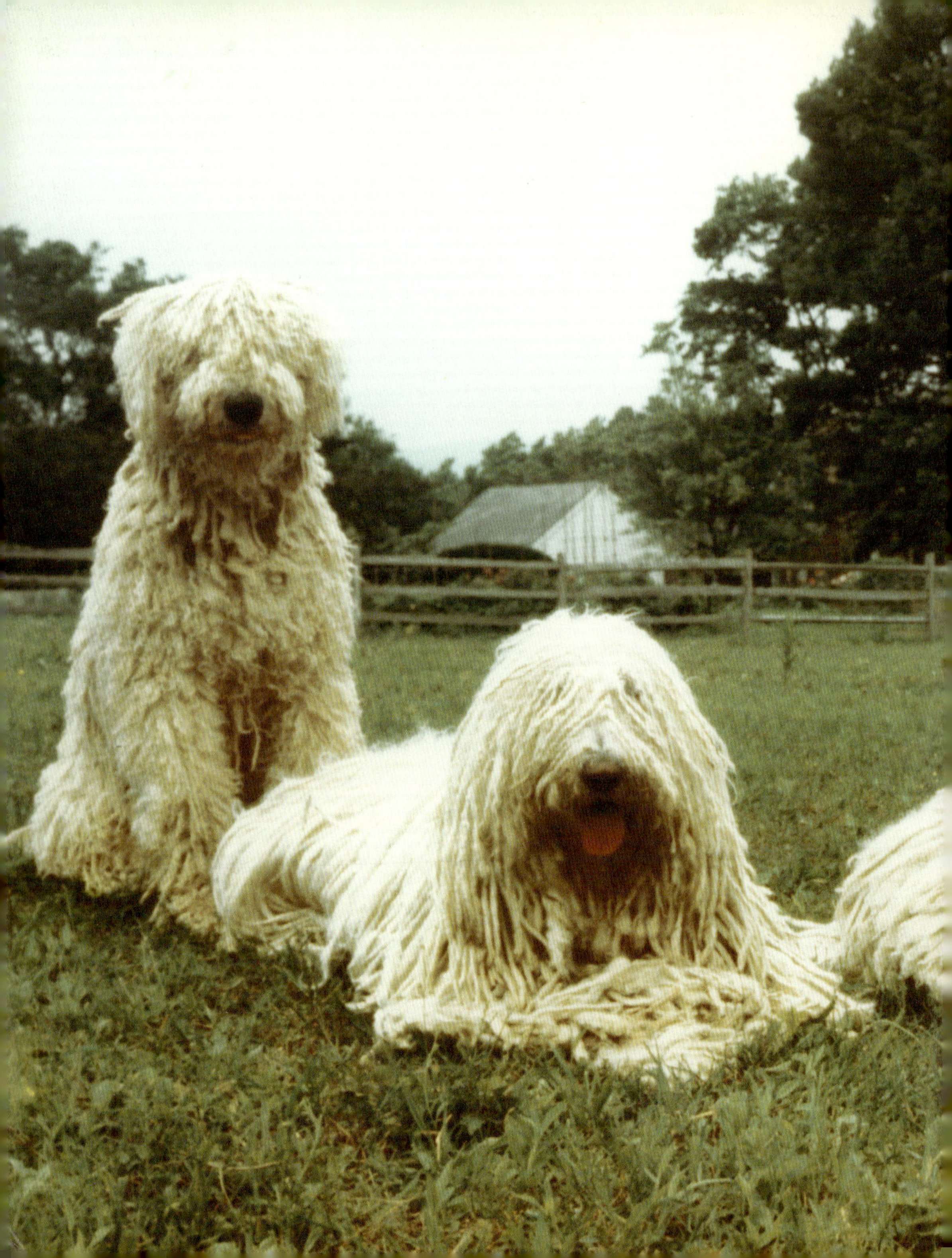

Komondor

By Joy C. Levy

Contents

8   History of the Komondor

Known as the "King of Hungarian Sheepdogs," the Komondor's existence can be traced back to the 12th century, when it arrived in Hungary with migrating herdsmen from the East. Follow the Komondor's storied history and learn about this unique-looking and talented flock guardian, including his development and establishment in Hungary. Special sections on the breed in the US and in media are also featured.

22   Characteristics of the Komondor

At first glance, the Komondor is a remarkable sight with his formidable size and striking corded coat, but there's much more than meets the eye! This is an independent dog bred to make decisions on his own. Read actual accounts of the breed's alertness and protective nature. Learn all about the breed's personality, temperament, breeding and whelping and important health considerations.

36   Breed Standard for the Komondor

Learn the requirements of a well-bred Komondor by studying the description of the breed set forth in the American Kennel Club and FCI standards. Both show dogs and pets must possess key characteristics as outlined in the breed standards.

46   Your Puppy Komondor

Find out about how to locate a well-bred Komondor puppy. Discover which questions to ask the breeder and what to expect when visiting the litter. Prepare for your puppy-accessory shopping spree. Also discussed are home safety, the first trip to the vet, socialization and solving basic puppy problems.

68   Proper Care of Your Komondor

Cover the specifics of taking care of your Komondor every day: feeding for the puppy, adult and senior dog; grooming, including coat care, ears, eyes, nails, teeth and bathing; and exercise needs for your dog. Also discussed are the essentials of dog ID and boarding.

Training Your Komondor   89

By Bardi McLennan
Begin with the basics of training the puppy and adult dog. Learn the principles of house-training the Komondor, including the use of crates and basic scent instincts. Get started by introducing the pup to his collar and leash and progress to the basic commands. Learn helpful hints that every owner should know when training a Komondor.

Healthcare of Your Komondor   113

By Lowell Ackerman DVM, DACVD
Become your dog's healthcare advocate and a well-educated canine keeper. Select a skilled and able veterinarian. Discuss breed-specific health issues, pet insurance, vaccinations and infectious diseases, the neuter/spay decision and a sensible, effective plan for parasite control, including fleas, ticks and worms.

Showing Your Komondor   144

Step into the center ring and find out about the world of showing pure-bred dogs. Here's how to get started in AKC shows, how they are organized and what's required for your dog to become a champion. Take a leap into the realms of obedience trials, agility and tracking tests.

Index.........156

KENNEL CLUB BOOKS® KOMONDOR
ISBN: 1-59378-378-7

Copyright © 2007 • Kennel Club Books, LLC • 308 Main Street, Allenhurst, NJ 07711 USA
Cover Design Patented: US 6,435,559 B2 • Printed in South Korea

All rights reserved. No part of this book may be reproduced in any form, by photostat, scanner, microfilm, xerography or any other means, or incorporated into any information retrieval system, electronic or mechanical, without the written permission of the copyright owner.

Library of Congress Cataloging-in-Publication Data
Levy, Joy C.
  Komondor / by Joy Levy.
      p. cm.
  ISBN 1-59378-378-7
  1. Komondor. I. Title.
  SF429.K65L47 2006
  636.7'3--dc22   2006011591

10 9 8 7 6 5 4 3 2 1

Photography by Carol Ann Johnson
with additional photos by:

Animal Photography/Sally Anne Thompson, Mary Bloom, Paulette Braun, Callea Photo, Carolina Biological Supply, Walter Chandoha, Crezentia, Juliette Cunliffe, Isabelle Français, Frank Garwood, Earl Graham, Stephen Green-Armytage, Mr. & Mrs. H. Richey Johnston, Bill Jonas, Bernard W. Kernan, Dr. Dennis Kunkel, Joy Levy, Tam C. Nguyen, Diane Pearce, Phototake, Jean Claude Revy, Michael Trafford and Alice van Kempen.

Illustrations by Patricia Peters.

HISTORY OF THE KOMONDOR

THE "KING" OF HUNGARY
Hungary has a distinguished set of dogs it calls its own. Currently, four of these breeds have been recognized in the United States by the American Kennel Club (AKC); these are the Komondor, Kuvasz, Puli and Viszla. All four were recognized and accepted into the AKC's stud register in the 1930s, though there were very few of the dogs in the country at that time. Hungary has several more "national breeds"—the Pumi, Mudi, Agar and Kopo, and Hungary also divides the Vizsla into two coat types, smooth and wire-haired; the latter is not recognized by the AKC. Among all of the native breeds, only the Komondor is spoken of as the "king."

A typical adult Komondor of the 1930s. Note the difference between this coat and that of Komondors today.

History

The history of the Komondor is assumed to be very long, though pedigrees have been kept formally only since 1924 in Hungary. The breed is usually said to have come into Hungary with the Magyars and to have been domesticated and at work in the 12th century. The Komondor was, and still is, a large dog used to guard flocks or herds of large animals. Originally the breed's charges were the unruly and semi-wild Racka, the large Hungarian sheep that grazed long ago on the Hungarian *puszta* (plains). The dogs are elemental livestock guard dogs who live with their flocks and guard them from predators, both four-legged and two-legged. Since the Komondor's coat so perfectly mimics the coats of his original charges, it is often hard to distinguish the dog from the sheep in the midst of a flock.

Irene Evers, an award-winning Hungarian breeder, in her splendid book *Our National Treasure: The Hungarian Komondor,* wrote that if you ask the Komondor, he will tell you where he came from. The dog loves cold weather, and his coat and paws seem made for it. He dislikes rain, she says, because it was rare where he came from. The area had little cloud cover, and the Komondor was well served by the nice hair-curtain that shielded his eyes from the brilliant winter

A flock guardian by trade, the Komondor is a natural protector of livestock. Here is Kiraly, working with sheep at the Adams ranch in Texas. Owners, Buster and Henny Adams.

KOMONDOR

RELATED BREEDS

The Komondor is probably closely related to the South Russian Ovcharka. The coats of the two breeds both cord, as does that of the Puli. The Puli, of course, is a herding dog, while the Komondor is a livestock guard dog. The temperaments of all the livestock guard dogs are very similar. These breeds include the Kuvasz, Maremma Sheepdog, Great Pyrenees, Tibetan Mastiff, Anatolian Shepherd Dog and more. Another breed with a coat that will remind you of a Komondor is the Bergamasco. An Italian breed whose coat forms flocks instead of cords, this herder is medium-sized. The coat does not feel like a Komondor coat, and the coat is somewhat different on different parts of the Bergamasco's body.

Maremma Sheepdog

Kuvasz

Puli

South Russian Ovcharka

History

sunshine. She concludes that his original home was rather dry and cold, with rapid changes of temperature and lots of sunshine. She says it had to be the Himalayas.

Dr. Zsigmond Katsányi, a great advocate for the Komondor in Hungary, believed that the dogs most probably arrived in Hungary in 1239, when 40,000 Kun tribesmen migrated into the Tisza regions with their families and herds and settled there. Zoltán Kenéz, in his 1922 book *The Komondor Defined,* says that it was word-of-mouth testimony among shepherds in the Kunsag region that both the Komondor and the Kuvasz were brought in by the Kuns in the 13th century. He felt that the Komondor was closely related to the South Russian Ovcharka, a sheepdog that also has matted hair, is often white and has dark pigment. Dr. Katsányi believed that the dogs we call Komondors began their journey in the Northern Himalayas, Bokhara, Uzbekistan. The Komondor went through the Ukraine, the Voronezh and the Volga region, the Northern Caucasus. These areas make up the shepherd's passage to the West.

No Hungarian discussion of the breed omits mention of Dr. Emil Raitsis, who wrote the first Hungarian Komondor breed standard, which was adopted in 1924. He wrote: "The Hungarian Komondor's ancestral character,

The first Komondor shown in England, Ohegyi Abrand Duna at Borgvaale. Bred by Ferenc Lehoczky, owned by Mrs. Pat Lanz.

THE KOMONDOR IN ENGLAND

The first imports into England belonged to Pat Lanz, an eminent Rottweiler and Puli breeder. Her first Komondor, a bitch, came from Hungary, and imports from the United States followed. The first litter was from a Hungarian bitch and an American male, but they unfortunately produced only a single litter with three beautiful puppies. The population in England is small; there is little demand for the dogs for work. A few are seen at the shows. A lovely bitch, Hercegvaros Cica of Borvaale and Loakespark, belonged to Ann Davis (now Ann Arch) and was a favorite at the shows in the 1970s. There have been other imports into the UK from Belgium and Hungary.

A lovely eight-month-old bitch, Zobraki Highland Spirit, owned by Mrs. Jackie Ferrigan.

Sire of the first Komondor litter in England, Hercegvaros Csupor at Borgvaale.

his exterior, which commands respect, fits exactly with the character of the true Hungarian. The honest character of these Hungarian people who still till the soil with back-breaking work led them to choose this dog as a companion. A freedom-loving people learned to value them and love them."

The name "Komondor" first appeared in print in 1544 in Peter Kakonyi's history of King Astiagis. This comes in a sentence: "the Komondor followed him, barking." The breed is mentioned by Amos Comenius in 1673 as "guarding the herd," and there are some descriptions of the Komondor in literature as early as 1653. Ferenc Pethe in his *Natural History* in 1815 not only described the Komondor and called him "leader of the dogs" but he also even printed a picture, which is often reproduced today; it does look like our contemporary dogs.

THE KOMONDOR IN THE US

The first dogs exported from Hungary to the United States went to individuals who had connections to Hungary and to a few eccentrics who prized the dogs for the temperaments they had read about—the dogs were unspoiled guard dogs and companions, loyal and brave. The first registered pair in the US belonged to Dr. Tibor de Cholnoky, a plastic surgeon. The next pair belonged to Mrs. William H. Sudduth III. These dogs were not prolific and the lines died out. During World War II, relations between the Hungarian Kennel Club and the AKC were suspended. Dogs imported in the late 1950s and 1960s fared better. Dixie Evans in Ohio acquired dogs from Germany and Hungary through Mrs. R.D. McLellan of Canada, and a few of these dogs can still be found in pedigrees of Komondors today.

Oscar Beregi in California

imported Hattyu, his first Komondor, in 1964, and this dog became the first American champion. Dogs imported to the Midwest and East Coast in the 1960s began serious showing. By the 1970s some established breeders emerged, and the dogs were being shown with some regularity. Szentivani Ingo, a dog imported in 1967 by the author's husband Marion J. Levy, Jr., a professor at Princeton University, was shown in the East, and he became the first Komondor to win a Working Group and then a Best in Show. He actually was rated among the top-ten show dogs all-breeds in the United States in 1972. Amazingly, he was shown with a corded coat, and his popularity in the show ring influenced other breeds, some corded, and some just other rare breeds.

Only later did people seek Komondors as prestige items; the unusual coat of the mature dog made the Komondor seem exotic. By the 1970s there was a commercial breeder in the Midwest and one on the East Coast, the latter importing two litters from Hungary.

We've mentioned Oscar Beregi, owner of the first AKC champion Komondor, Hattyu. A Hungarian actor and the son of a very famous Hungarian Shakespearian actor, Beregi finished Hattyu's championship in 1965. Beregi was president of the first Komondor club, the Komondor Club of America, which was founded in 1967. Marion Levy was the first president of the second Komondor club, the Middle Atlantic States Komondor Club (MASKC). This

Hungarian through and through, this Kom fits right in with this young lady in traditional Hungarian garb at a Budapest show.

Ch. Hattyu, first Komondor champion in the US, owned by Oscar Beregi.

Hercegvaros Cica of Borgvaale and Loakespark, imported by Mrs. Pat Lanz and owned by Mrs. Ann Arch. This lovely bitch made history for the breed in England, where she won many awards in Rare-Breeds and Breed classes. Worldwide she became known as "Kitten," the translation of her Hungarian name "Cica."

club was founded in 1973 after a dust-up with the Komondor Club of America over whether the dogs should be required to have corded coats. Though it is a regional club, the MASKC serves the dogs all over the US and probably has more connections with foreign clubs than the national club. As in most dog breeds, the clubs are often at odds with each other! Both clubs have newsletters. The Middle Atlantic States Komondor Club also publishes books and pamphlets relating to the Komondor.

Some celebrities have owned Komondors in the US, though mostly very briefly. Gene Tunney, the former heavyweight boxing champion, got one of the first dogs registered in the US as a house guard at the height of the publicity over the kidnapping of the Lindbergh baby. The opera singer Maria Jeritza had a litter, although they do not appear as registered in the AKC stud register. More recently, Zsa Zsa Gabor owned a pair, though only briefly. She was given a pair named Jancsika and Juliska (in a Hungarian fairy tale, Jancsika and Juliska occupy a

History

place similar to that of Hansel and Gretel). Oscar Beregi took these dogs into rescue. The bitch went to a pet home, but the dog, Ch. Fouti Hercules Jancsika, went to John and Carol Kincel and had a worthy show career.

It was not until the 1970s that farmers and ranchers wanted Komondors for their traditional work—as flock guardians, good for combating predators like wolves, coyotes, cougars, bears or the neighbors' dogs. Thanks to an unusually fine working Komondor named Maggie, owned by Buster and Henny Adams in Evant, Texas, and the rising interest in livestock guard dogs in general in the United States and Canada, working Komondors have been a big success on the North American continent. Raymond Coppinger, who founded Hampshire College's Livestock Dog Project in 1977, a project using livestock guard dogs for predator control, wrote in his book *Dogs* that Maggie was the first livestock guard dog he saw actually protecting Angora goats from coyotes and bobcats. Credit must go to Coppinger for explaining the role of livestock guard dogs to the United States Department of Agriculture (USDA), as well as to ranchers and farmers in the US and Canada. Livestock guard dogs are used now with sheep, cattle, goats, emus, poultry, etc.

Unfortunately quite a number of working Komondors are not registered, and there seem to be many Komondor crosses. These are often crosses between Komondors and Great Pyrenees. The dogs are sometimes used on small farms but more often with large flocks or herds, with several dogs working together. Some show breeders refuse to supply dogs for work. Others supply them and earnestly encourage owners of working dogs to have x-rays done on their dogs to make sure that they are free of orthopedic problems if they plan to breed them and also to be sure to register the puppies. It would indeed be a shame if the work done in Hungary to keep the Komondor a pure breed was not honored in the United States.

The first AKC standard for the breed was adopted in 1937; it was

Here is Ch. Indian Run Acel Ropi, a beautiful example of an American-bred Kom.

KOMONDOR

based on the 1936 Hungarian standard by Abonyi, Anghi and Mueller. The standard has been revised three times: in 1971, in 1973 and, most recently, in 1994. The 1971 standard did not require the Komondor to be corded, and this created a split among Komondor fanciers. Initially the dogs in the US were shown with their coats brushed out. Probably Marion Levy's greatest contribution to the breed was his insistence on showing Ch. Szentivani Ingo (known as "Duna") with a fully corded coat.

Marion and Joy Levy with Ch. Boytar-Hercegvaros Bocs.

NUMBER OF KOMONDORS INDIVIDUALLY REGISTERED BY THE AMERICAN KENNEL CLUB 1937–2004

1937	2	1960	1	1983	138
1938	0	1961	1	1984	192
1939	2	1962	12	1985	170
1940	1	1963	3	1986	178
1941	0	1964	12	1987	170
1942	0	1965	15	1988	174
1943	1	1966	19	1989	180
1944	0	1967	14	1990	165
1945	0	1968	38	1991	202
1946	0	1969	34	1992	197
1947	0	1970	54	1993	224
1948	0	1971	73	1994	163
1949	0	1972	103	1995	180
1950	0	1973	121	1996	160
1951	0	1974	100	1997	123
1952	0	1975	103	1998	103
1953	0	1976	99	1999	112
1954	0	1977	99	2000	81
1955	0	1978	87	2001	85
1956	0	1979	102	2002	65
1957	0	1980	135	2003	69
1958	1	1981	156	2004	84
1959	0	1982	128	2005	76

Through his perseverance, the AKC finally agreed to change the Komondor standard in 1973 to require a Komondor to be corded by the age of two years. The ring success of this one dog not only changed the appearance of the Komondor but also probably changed the appearance of the Puli. In the 1970s most Pulik were shown with their coats brushed out, but now you almost never see a Puli in the ring without cords.

The Komondor has always been rare in the US. Only 282 dogs were registered with the AKC between 1937 and 1971, and 1971 marked a high point with 73 dogs registered. The registrations after that increased to as high as 224 in 1993. The most litters (66) were registered in 1992. After that, registrations of both individual dogs and litters began to decline, and in recent years the Komondor has had the lowest registration numbers among the breeds in the Working Group. The Komondor is hardly a prolific breed. It is probably fortunate that this is so, since the breed's limited numbers make it difficult for unscrupulous breeders and irresponsible owners to acquire Komondors.

We know that the Komondor originally came to Hungary as a dog used to protect livestock. Additionally the breed has been used in Hungary for protecting property and factories as well as for police work. It is hardly possible for a dog working in a remote area or on a ranch to be cleaned up and taken to an American dog show, as has been done in Hungary. Working dogs' coats may have patches missing, and they may be dirty beyond any possibility of getting them clean enough to show to US judges. Dogs working alone on their own property might also display a temperament that would not be acceptable in the ring to judges in the US. These

A splendid Komondor bitch, Ch. Kurcafuredi-Subas Edi with the Twin Towers in the background.

Winning Best of Breed at the 1989 Trenton Kennel Club Dog Show, Ch. Boytar-Hercegvaros Balna.

A GREAT HUNGARIAN BREEDER

Irene Evers with two of her favorite Komondors, Hunor and Puszta.

Mrs. Evers judging Ch. Trentvaros A. Koda in Princeton at a MASKC gathering.

The breeder of the first AKC Best in Show Komondor, Ch. Szentivani Ingo (Duna), was Irene Evers, an amazing Hungarian gold-medal breeder. She originally bred under the kennel name Szentivani; then, when she did breeding at a cooperative for the government, she used the kennel name Mount Everest. At the end of her life, she returned to the Szentivani name. She also wrote a book entitled *Our National Treasure: The Hungarian Komondor*, which has been published in English. This book, translated by a number of people who really cared about Mrs. Evers and the Komondor breed, has never been published in Hungary, although Irene offered the manuscript there and in other European countries. This author did send the Hungarian manuscript to the Hungarian Komondor Club and gave them permission to print the book, but this has not happened. I hope it eventually does appear in Hungarian. Mrs. Evers did not live to see the finished book, but we printed it in chapters in the Middle Atlantic States Komondor Club newsletter. Duna, the six-month-old puppy she sent to an unknown couple in the US, Mr. and Mrs. Marion J. Levy, Jr., certainly made a big difference to the Komondor breed in this country. Mrs. Evers came to the US to judge on one historical occasion and was able to see some of Duna's many champion and (soon to be) champion offspring.

DUNA IN CORDS

One of the most important sires in the breed is still Ch. Szentivani Ingo, whom we called Duna. He was the first Komondor to win an all-breed Best in Show, and most important, we exhibited him in a corded coat. Before 1973, it was permitted to show a Komondor brushed out, something most Komondor owners deplored. Komondors were always shown with corded coats in Europe. Despite the lectures we got from judges, we insisted on cording his coat and showing him. He was such an impressive dog, and he had such a good coat, that when he was a mature dog, his quality was undeniable.

Because of Duna and his persuasive owner, the author's husband, Marion J. Levy, Jr., the AKC finally accepted a standard that requires the coat to be corded by the age of two years. This actually affected the Kom's Hungarian cousin, the Puli, as well as the Komondor. Because of Duna's success in the show ring, more and more Pulik were shown corded.

Duna at seven years old winning the breed from the Veteran Class.

Duna and some of his offspring and friends get together at a MASKC match.

Duna at a dog show in Boston—from the *Boston Globe*.

Ch. Indian Run Az Aranyos Chimera demonstrating her winning ways in 2004.

Ch. Lajosmegyi Dahu Digal, taking Best in Show at the Seattle Kennel Club Dog Show.

dogs object to being touched by strangers, especially strange judges who may not like them. Their behavior might well be considered too aggressive. The worth of such working dogs cannot be measured by or dignified with show titles. Out in all weather, ever-vigilant and trustworthy, they retain the same qualities that the Hungarian shepherds bred into their dogs long ago. May it always be so.

THE BREED IN MEDIA

There are few books on the breed, and some of the best are not in English. In Hungary a book by Ócsag Imre and Pál Sarkány on the Hungarian breeds has been translated into English. First published as *The Dogs of Hungary* in 1977, then reprinted as *Hungarian Dog Breeds* in 1987, it is now out of print. The Middle Atlantic States Komondor Club published Irene Evers's book *Our National Treasure: The Hungarian Komondor* in English in 1990; unfortunately it has not yet been published in Hungarian. In France, Laurent and Anna Racz-Caroff published a beautiful book with exceptional, lovely photos. This is *Un Chien Incroyable: le Komondor et les*

Angyal's Espuela Magyar, the famous "Maggie," who appeared on the cover of the *Smithsonian* magazine and was featured in *Life* magazine. Owners, Buster and Henny Adams.

autres bergers Hongroise (*An Incredible Dog: The Komondor and the Other Hungarian Shepherd Dogs*), published in 1984. The text was translated into English by the MASKC in 1991. A charming book was written in 1922 and privately printed in only 100 copies in Hungarian by Zoltán Kenéz; it was reprinted with the original Hungarian text and an English translation by the MASKC in 1992. The Middle Atlantic States Komondor Club publishes booklets and pamphlets on the Komondor at work as well, including Henny Adams's wonderful *Diary of Maggie* (1980), the diary of that first American Komondor who worked so successfully with livestock.

Two videos were produced to illustrate the 1973 AKC standard. One was made by the AKC; the other was made by Robert Halmi, a movie and video personality who was Hungarian, had several Komondors and was for a time president of the Komondor Club of America. This second video has shots of good dogs in action, including shots of dogs at work in Canada and on farms in Hungary. The footage is outstanding.

CHARACTERISTICS OF THE KOMONDOR

PERSONALITY AND TEMPERAMENT

What is a Komondor like? To start with, his appearance is unique—nothing else looks like this large white dog with a corded coat. While it is normal to say his character is unique, this is not really true. You can find a very similar temperament in quite a number of other livestock guard breeds, including the Great Pyrenees, Kuvasz, Maremma Sheepdog, Anatolian Shepherd and Tibetan Mastiff. All of these breeds were originally bred by shepherds to guard livestock. They were not bred to be house dogs. Their size alone makes them unsuitable for apartment living, and they are not likely to be docile pets. They were bred to be independent thinkers, and you can translate that to mean "stubborn mules." They want to make their own decisions about what they guard, how they guard and from whom they will take orders.

In 1975 I wrote an article on Komondor temperament. My findings were based on my experiences with my first Komondor, Duna. I have had many Komondors since then, but none have been as amazing as he was. That dog ended up having not only a spectacular show career but also a wonderful life as a beloved character in our town. My veterinarian, who was also fond of Duna, always told us that most other owners would have gotten rid of the dog when he was a puppy. I observed a similar learning process in Texas with Maggie, the first Komondor who was successfully used as a livestock guard dog in the US. That was a case of Angora-goat breeders who got the dog because they had lost most of their kids (young goats)

Beyond his unique appearance, the Komondor is extremely loyal to and a unmatched protector of his "flock," whether the flock is four-legged or two-legged.

Characteristics

to coyotes and were willing to try a livestock guard dog. Maggie belonged to Buster and Henny Adams, and Henny kept a diary of her progress (the aforementioned *Diary of Maggie*), which should be required reading for people using Komondors for work. Like us, the Adamses learned from their first Komondor, who was not at all like their previous German Shepherds. Those dogs ended up killing goats and sheep instead of guarding them. The year after Maggie came, no kids were lost to coyotes, but Maggie insisted on guarding "her way."

I refined my thoughts on temperament after a trip to Hungary, but I must tell you that Dr. Zsigmond Katsányi, the then grand old man of Komondor breeders, told me after he read my article that he was surprised that it had been written by someone who was not Hungarian. So I guess I learned a lot about Hungarians as well as about Komondors from Duna!

To describe Komondor temperament, I must draw heavily on that first article. Basically I see the breed as a formidable guard and a loyal companion. Your first sight of a Komondor could be that of a large white animal standing alone on a rise of ground he has selected carefully because it commands a view of all possible points of entry for intruders. A rough thick coat of felty tassels hangs to the ground.

Koms who grow up with children form a special bond with their human "siblings."

Above the large mass of his body, his head is carried proud and erect, with ears pitched to hear the slightest strange sound. Though heavy hair covers the eyes and ears, no one can mistake the watchful, listening attitude of the dog. Lonely, majestic and silent, he watches over his flock.

Or you might see several large Komondors lying in the shade of a

Joy Levy calls Ch. Boytar-Da-Co-Tah Atok up the steps on the Princeton University campus.

tree behind great iron gates. The male is a lion surrounded by his pride, and young puppies play as older bitches watch over them. It is a peaceful, happy family, but as if signaled by an unseen hand, the grown dogs are at the gate, barking to announce the approach of a stranger.

Or, on a farm, a large ragged dog is tied to a tree. He lies in the dust made by his pacing a circle at the end of his rope. The tree has been chosen so that no one can reach the front door without crossing that dusty circle. No lock is needed on that door. The dog barks, bares his teeth and snarls as strangers approach, and the owner warns you that you cannot touch him, even though you are not afraid.

I am not Hungarian. I was not brought up with a Komondor who loved me when I was a child. I am always interested to see that a Hungarian who has owned a Komondor will come and look at our dogs from a distance. They do not touch them or make a move toward them. They expect them to be unfriendly. They wait until the dog goes up to them and sniffs them, perhaps even extends a paw, which our dogs usually do when approached in this manner.

"They expect a Komondor to be unfriendly." This is the key. To an American, a Komondor looks like a huge children's toy. Often an American will say that he cannot believe that anything that looks as

> **KOMONDORS ON AND OFF DUTY**
> The Komondor is not a restless dog. When there is no job to be done, he is a quiet companion. Many farmers say Komondors are the "laziest dogs" they ever had. This is misleading, as a Komondor can spring into action with explosive power. When you ask a farmer if he has had losses of stock with the Komondor there, he says no! Usually quiet by day, the Komondor patrols his property at night. He is the original night watchman. A working dog barks at night to warn predators that he is on duty. Ranchers and farmers are glad to hear the Komondor bark—it means that he is on duty.

"sweet" as that can be a guard dog. Even some owners (usually novices with young dogs) announce cheerfully that their dog "loves everyone!" They are often sure that their handling and their affection toward the dog has made this the case. I guess I should not have been surprised when told in Budapest that a man on the street or at a dog show in Hungary can make the same estimation that Americans can. The Komondor is also rare in Hungary, and no longer better understood by the layman in his homeland than he is abroad.

The American standard says that the dog is "wary of strangers." It describes an excellent house guard: earnest, courageous and faithful. "It is devoted to its master and will defend him from attack by any stranger." The Hungarian standard (official English translation) says that the Komondor's exterior and behavior rouse respect, astonishment and fear. It calls the dog "mistrustful" and describes a powerful animal who watches and guards his own area and herd and attacks boldly without a cry. Does this sound terrible to an American? It shouldn't, if you consider what this working dog's job is supposed to be. He is a guard dog and a dog used to guard the large semi-wild sheep of the Hungarian plain. He was bred to protect the flock, family and property against predators and thieves. Moreover, he was bred to be a decision-making, responsibility-taking dog. He was truly in charge of the flock; in the absence of a human shepherd, it was up to the Komondor to decide how far to go and when to return home, as well as to watch over and protect his charges from marauding beasts and thieves.

WHAT CONSTITUTES GOOD TEMPERAMENT IN A KOMONDOR?

Obviously he must be courageous and aggressive in the sense that he has no fear. There must be no suggestion of shyness about the dog. This does not mean that he should be vicious; a Komondor is surprisingly alert and inquisitive for a large working dog. He lies in a characteristic guarding position with feet tucked firmly under him so that he can spring instantly into effective action. He seems never to sleep. He goes up readily to all strange things, confronting them boldly but attacking only when he feels that his property or his people are in some way threatened. He makes his decision as to what constitutes a threat independently and then acts with confidence and authority. In short, he is an independent thinker and a splendid companion to have guarding your flock.

I cannot speak of good temperament without getting immediately into situations where Komondor behavior borders on the unacceptable. Obviously, things can and do go wrong. I would like to discuss some of these things because this breed now exists in modern American society, and the dog's formerly "forbidding" exterior seems now to appeal to many people who are not familiar with

Komondors are very comfortable with any livestock. Here is Ch. Hercegvaros Ergike with a handsome equine pal.

the dog's character. I would like to tell three stories about Komondors—I quote them as they were told by proud owners:

"Duna is a neighborhood hero. He roused us at 4 A.M. with insistent barking and, though reprimanded, refused to quiet down until he led my husband to the fence just in time to see flames burst from the top of a building across the way. As a result, we turned in an alarm that saved the field house from total destruction. It was a cold, foggy night and only Duna's sensitive nose and responsible behavior as an intelligent working dog resulted in such prompt control of a serious fire."

"I was running, slipped and fell. As people approached to help me, writhing in pain on the grass, Oh-M braced himself, guarding me against at least a dozen would-be helpers. A word from me, in an unkind tone, no doubt, brought him to me. With a short wag, he approached me as if to see if I was really in a condition to make important decisions. Another word brought a nose-poke in the ear as if to say, 'Well, you're acting a little weird, but I guess you're still lucid,' and the people were allowed to pick me up and take me to the hospital."

"He [Diosgyori Herceg Kajla] was the most excellent protector of house and person. Some years ago a robber with a weapon attacked me in our big house that stands alone. The neighbors lived far away; I was alone in the house. It was 10 P.M. The dog, in a special danger-signaling voice, started to bark. He was shaking in every joint with rage. I tried to calm him, but he did not listen to me and jumped over the fence and caught a man—the man fired a shot but missed me. The dog rushed at him, pushed him to the ground and placed his mouth on his throat. In this position he held the robber from 10 P.M. until 2 A.M., when the police came from Budapest. [The police] then captured the robber, whom the dog did not wish to release in any way." (Translated from Hungarian.)

The first dog was mine. The second was officially Mount Everest Bitang, who lived in Brooklyn with owner Saul Danoff. The third was a Hungarian dog who belonged to Irene Evers. He sired many litters and his name appears in many of our pedigrees. I

A handsome watchdog, Ch. Varhegy Hunor.

think that his spirit lives on, too.

Wonderful stories—wonderful dogs. No trace of shyness here, nor of unprovoked viciousness. I gather that even Diosgyori Herceg Kajla did not seriously harm the burglar with the weapon, and Oh-M allowed strangers to intervene when he realized it would help his master. But in all three cases the dog's first instinct was to make the decisions; all refused to meekly let the master make the choices. Duna knew that the fire was wrong and disobeyed commands in order to alert us. Oh-M first kept help away until he was sure that their intentions were honorable. Kajla knew that the man was an enemy and didn't want to release him to strangers. These dogs have an active, positive approach in their thinking that goes along with a big, physical dog.

I have described Komondor temperament as being alert and watchful and the dog as an independent thinker, a

Provided that they are properly introduced and socialized, Koms enjoy the companionship of other dogs.

Characteristic of the species, few dogs will turn down table scraps. It is not recommended to indulge the beggar because a balanced diet can easily be "unbalanced" by extras.

The Komondor was bred to guard flocks and herds of large animals. Puppies typically exhibit their protective nature at a young age.

decision-making, responsibility-taking guard. What is this beast like in the US where he tends no sheep and cannot find a wolf? How does the Komondor behave, and how is his behavior received?

He is born just as alert and watchful as his Hungarian counterpart. He attaches himself with the same loyalty and devotion to his family and property. He needs human companionship and an orderly routine. A puppy is immediately devoted and accepts the house-training routine with incredible ease. In his own surroundings he is playful, humorous and, above all, full of love. A Komondor wants to be with his master, not just in the same house but in the same room and preferably by his side, where he by choice will lean on his master. He prefers to eat in the kitchen, and he likes for his master to be with him when he eats. If any member of the family is away, the dog is restless and wants to lie by the door, awaiting the return of the stray; he wants all of his family at home where he can watch them. This means that he is a poor kennel dog. He will transfer with difficulty to a kennel environment, especially if he is not very young.

He needs a lot of socialization, being handled by many different people if he is later to be in contact with many people. And he needs a family to attach himself to. By six months of age, a Komondor can be loyal and devoted to the point where you begin to worry about him. Every member of the household is included in his devotion—the children, the cleaning woman, any regular visitors and the other animals, including dogs, cats, birds, anything. Even a young dog has a terrific sense of property, and an older one is almost pathological on the subject. If there is a fence, the fence is the boundary. If no fence exists, the property is tracked and an imaginary fence is erected and guarded. If there is a fence, the guarding is a noisy affair; no strange vehicle or living thing can approach day or night without the Komondor announcing it with loud barking. As the dog matures, usual traffic is ignored, but a truck at night on a street where trucks usually come only by day, a strange bicycle that is not ordinarily in the neighborhood, a dog that is not a habitual passerby, etc., cause the alarm to be sounded. Your house is truly safe. So is the family car, and it is not to be assaulted by a gas-station attendant with a weapon (the gas hose or a windshield rag). Almost every Komondor owner has rips in his upholstery and deep scratches on the inside of his car from his Kom's reaction to this perceived assault.

How, then, do you live with a Komondor? If you have taken one into your home or are contemplating getting one, the first thing to realize is that this beast, especially the male, is a lot of dog to handle, for at least two reasons. First, the Komondor is a big, powerful dog. Second, this breed has been bred successfully to be a decision-making animal. The Komondor decides who is the enemy and protects his possessions from danger in whatever way he sees fit. Any male must be obedience-trained before one year of age if he is to be managed by more than one person. I do not mean that competitive obedience awards are required; I mean that the dog must be taught to heel, sit, lie down, stay and come on command. For example, if you leave the dog with a cleaning woman or a babysitter, the dog has to take direction from these people as well as from you. We find that even with obedience training, we cannot let our dog run without a leash unless we are in a really isolated area or unless one person devotes his full attention to controlling the dog. If the Komondor is running free, he can be restrained from investigating something only if you see it before he does and call him before he gets a head start. If he sights the "enemy" first, forget it unless you can outrun him.

Duna happened to really like people. His "attacks" were almost always on animals. It is not by chance that he liked people. Again, like many guard dogs, a Komondor usually likes only people he knows. If you want to keep a Komondor friendly, you must be sure that he "knows" a lot of people. Most

Koms are very affectionate dogs with people they are familiar with, responding positively to loving attention and approval from their owners.

Komondors like children and put up with a great deal from (even unfamiliar) children, though unfamiliar adults are not tolerated lightly. On the other hand, individual dogs vary as to how physical their "warning" is. One dog protecting his child's wagon from my child warned my child by pulling him away with teeth that tore a shirt and bruised flesh. Dogs that are displeased often bare their teeth and approach with open mouths in a way that causes their teeth to touch and bruise rather than bite. Occasionally dogs that are pleased also do this. One circumstance that is almost sure to lead to trouble is a Komondor with his food threatened. Unfortunately this can extend to his guarding a bone or a chew toy, which a Komondor inevitably treats as food.

Like all of the livestock guard dogs, Komondors should tolerate any animals that are yours. A working dog will cut out a new flock member but not harm it. They positively like cats, and cats like them as well. They are good with birds, from cockatiels to emus, and generally have no hunt and/or chase instincts. You can rarely get them to chase a squirrel or a deer. They like to watch other animals; they act as we do when we watch television. They are generally gentle with any young animals. Grown Komondors do not usually welcome strange canines on their property, though in some cases they fall in love with another animal—dog, cat, goat, etc.—and try to bring their friend home. They enjoy having a companion, whether it is another dog or a cat. An older dog is often rejuvenated by the entry of a younger dog into his life. People with working dogs find that an older Komondor will teach a younger one all of the rules. They certainly explain to youngsters that sheep or goats are not to be hassled. However, most breeders and owners find that raising two puppies at once has its problems. If you are using the dogs for work, they spend too much time playing with each other, and

Puppy socialization with little people ensures that the adult Komondor will respect children he knows.

Characteristics

The temperament and personality of the dam will be reflected in her progeny. Like begets like, and if you don't like the dam, you likely won't be happy with one of her pups.

if you are trying to raise show dogs, puppies can destroy each other's coats. Komondors are devoted forever to the people and animals they grow up with.

This is an alert dog, and he requires an alert master. Improper handling can occur in many situations with well-meaning owners, and the dog can then be suspected of having a bad temperament when he in reality does not. I know because we have made some mistakes ourselves. I do not mean to preach but rather to share some things we have learned. For example, incorrect handling can occur if you expect your Komondor to be a gentleman. This is a peasant—he mouths the things he loves as well as the things he hates. You are inevitably bruised by teeth and paws, and this cannot be easily avoided. Improper handling can occur if you do not give the dog a suitable job. If you fail to show him his duty, he will certainly make a job for himself, and you may not like the job he chooses.

You cannot let a Komondor get away with things you disapprove of, whether it is getting on the furniture, barking excessively, jumping up on people, etc. A firm hand on a choke collar and a strong back are required if you are to live comfortably with this breed.

Good breeders will have appropriate testing done to ensure to the best of their ability that they breed from healthy parents to produce healthy pups.

Incorrect handling can also occur if you do not listen to the dog or try to see the situation as he sees it. If you have a fence, you must realize that people, even children, climbing over it and running across your yard are truly in danger of being attacked. A fence should bear a "Beware of Dog" warning. If you do not have a fence, know that skiers on your mountain property look like trespassers to your Komondor, that men picking up your garbage look like thieves to your dog and that any repairmen working on your house look like burglars. A postman extending a package or a policeman extending a ticket to you looks like a man threatening the master, and an Alaskan Malamute gazing at your dog with naked eyes surely looks like a wolf. Protect your Komondor from accidental wrongdoing. He is only a good guard dog if you can interpret his messages.

Is any dog worth this effort? You bet the Komondor is. Ask any Komondor owner. Not only are we safe from the attacks of evil strangers but we can also trust our dogs to keep us safe from fire, report the smell of gas, tell us if appliances are not working, wake us if children are crying and we do not hear them, announce that an outside door has blown open, etc. If any of the other dogs (if you have a multi-dog household) have strayed, it is the Komondor who waits up for them and announces at least five minutes before they arrive at the door that they are coming and need welcoming. But this is only part of the comfort of having a Komondor. We find the companionship of this "King of the Hungarian Sheepdogs" much more interesting than that of a dog with a blander temperament. An obedience-trained Komondor represents a triumph of communication between man and dog and also represents something closely related to the taming of the elements or the wooing of a wild animal. A Komondor may want to fight the wolf, but in a real sense he is himself very close to the wolf. We would hate to see this kind of temperament and this unique breed disappear.

BREEDING AND WHELPING
Komondors breed best when the dogs live together; it is difficult to arrange breedings between Komondors who do not know

Characteristics

WHO'S THE BOSS?
Komondor males are very bossy with other males, and we do not recommend keeping two unaltered (unneutered) males together.

each other. Some bitches only come in heat once a year, and litters on the average are small. The AKC for years used a figure of 5.5 puppies as the average for a Komondor litter. There is a rather high degree of neonatal mortality, especially among breeders who use heating elements in the whelping box. The puppies do best without any heat; the dam's heavy coat means she is likely to become too hot if heating elements are used, and she does not like to stay with the puppies if too hot. In a cool room she will be an efficient and devoted dam.

We really do have breeding problems for quite a number of different reasons:

1. The adult Komondor is a large dog. He is not a giant dog, but he is too big for a grown man to pick up easily, so just handling the dogs can be a problem.
2. Komondors have a lot of hair. They have so much hair that when you breed a pair, the hair gets in the way. Some people tie the cords "out of the way," which is truly hard to do. Often the tails get in the way during the mating process when they tie.
3. Komondors are not easy breeders. They mature slowly. Bitches usually experience their first heat between one and two years of age. Some do not come in heat until well after two years old. They do not always have two heat cycles a year. Some have only one heat per year, and others have a cycle every eight months. Males are not always avid stud dogs. They suddenly become sensitive and will not push the bitch. They dislike strangers trying to help them.
4. The timing is often bizarre. We can never think 10–14 days. For some bitches the right time is 7

The corded coat of the Komondor will provide a comfortable respite and plenty of heat for her puppies.

More so than many other breeds, Komondors have their fair share of problems when it comes to breeding. When it is a success, though, what a lovely sight indeed!

Quality in a puppy shows at an early age, as exhibited by the future Ch. Javictreva Camaraderie.

days, for others as late as 21 days is right. Dogs are often not eager until the magic moment when the bitch is eager. More breedings are missed because owners think it is too late when it is actually too early. In my experience, artificial breeding with either chilled or frozen sperm presents a real challenge for timing properly.

5. Komondors are aggressive guard dogs. If a bitch comes to the dog and she growls at the dog's master, the Komondor may decide not to breed her. His loyalty is mainly to his owner. He will not breed a bitch he does not like!

6. A Komondor must be white. Everything that is not white (nose, eyes, pads, etc.) must be as dark as possible. It is really hard to get everything right!

So if you want to breed Komondors, you have to think about how difficult it can be.

When I asked my veterinarian about our breeding problems, he told me they were common to all rare breeds; indeed, this is why they are rare!

As for whelping, some bitches can do it all by themselves while others can decide they want help. Most will not tolerate help from people they don't know, although they all seem to understand that a veterinarian is a friend. Some have to be urged to let the puppies nurse. Some puppies figure it out despite their inefficient dams. All of the Komondor bitches I have seen end up being very devoted mothers. They can be quite aggressive in guarding when the puppies are very small.

By the time the puppies are being weaned, if you have other dogs, the dam often chooses a "babysitter" and turns the puppies over to a younger Komondor, sometimes a bitch, sometimes a male. Males are equally good at this job!

Puppies grow rapidly, and as soon as they can stand and get their heads down, they want and can manage food that is not gruel. An eight-week-old puppy is an avid eater and needs at least three meals a day. A good-sized Komondor should gain ten pounds a month (after the first month, when they do not usually weigh ten pounds yet) until about nine months of age, and then they slow down. Puppies eat a lot; grown dogs are maintained on much less than most big breeds. Komondors usually do not eat more than five cups of food a day as adults.

PRESERVING THE BREED

Middle Atlantic States Komondor Club (MASKC) member breeders prefer not to supply breeding pairs, wishing to preserve the breed as it has been for centuries and thus wanting to see only the best specimens bred. A dog can be a marvelous working dog, but if he has physical faults like poor hips, poor pigment, poor teeth, a bad coat, etc., it is preferable not to have him used for breeding. Any dog or bitch of unsuitable temperament should not be bred, even if he or she is a handsome physical specimen. Breeding unregistered dogs is frowned upon; the Hungarians worked very hard to get the dogs registered in order to preserve the breed. We should not disregard their effort. Many things cannot be predicted in any one puppy, and no one can responsibly predict that two puppies will grow up to be a suitable pair for breeding. If you start with one Komondor, and he or she turns out to be a great mature specimen, you should then, and only then, seek out the best possible mate for that particular animal. From a breeder's point of view, by that time you also will have learned more about the breed and will be in a better position to raise puppies properly than a novice. Acquire a Komondor because you want a Komondor and you value the characteristics that make the breed special, not to breed, raise and sell Komondors before you really know what they are like. Experienced breeders will tell you that breeding and raising these dogs is not easy. In Hungary they say that it requires money, money and more money. It is also easier to have the patience that is required if you start with a dog that you know to be your proven invaluable guard and companion.

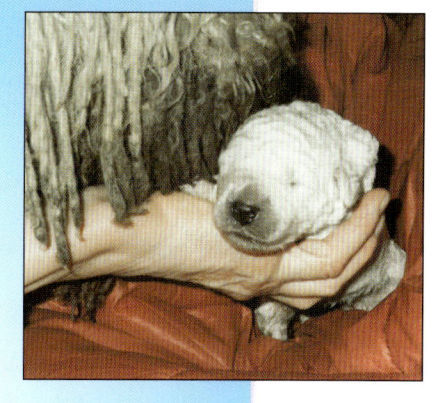

BREED STANDARD FOR THE

KOMONDOR

Dr. Emil Raitsis's book *A Magyar Kutyák* presented the first standard of the breed in 1922; it became the official standard in 1924 and remained in effect until 1935. Dr. Csaba Anghi wrote a less strict standard in 1936; it became known as the Abonyi, Anghi and Mueller standard and was in effect until 1960. In that year a new official standard was adopted, later slightly revised in 1966. In 2000 the Fédération Cynologique Internationale (FCI) adopted a new official standard, which is the current one in use in Hungary. It is posted on the website of the Hungarian Kennel Club.

A giant mountain of Komondor, Ch. Boytar-Da-Co-Tah Abba.

The first AKC standard was accepted in 1937, likely based on the 1936 standard, and it was revised in 1971 and again in 1973, then reformatted in 1994. First we present the AKC standard, followed by the FCI standard, translated from the Hungarian by the author with the assistance of Maria Zankowich and Dr. George Halasi-Kun.

THE AKC STANDARD FOR THE KOMONDOR

General Appearance: The Komondor is characterized by imposing strength, dignity, courageous demeanor and pleasing conformation. He is a large, muscular dog with plenty of bone and substance, covered with an unusual, heavy coat of white cords. The working Komondor lives during the greater part of the year in the open, and his coat serves to help him blend in with his flock and to protect him from extremes of weather and beasts of prey.

Nature and Characteristics: The Komondor is a flock guardian, not a herder. Originally

Ch. Szentivani Ingo, the first Komondor to win Best in Show in the US.

developed in Hungary to guard large herds of animals on the open plains, the Komondor was charged with protecting the herd by himself, with no assistance and no commands from his master. The mature, experienced dog tends to stay close to his charges, whether a flock or a family; he is unlikely to be drawn away from them in chase, and typically doesn't wander far. Though very sensitive to the desires of his master, heavy-handed training will produce a stubborn, unhappy Komondor. While reserved with strangers, the Komondor is demonstrative with those he loves, selflessly devoted to his family and his charges, and will defend them against any attack. The combination of this devotion to all things dear to him and the desire to take responsibility for them produces an excellent guardian of herds or home, vigilant, courageous and very faithful.

Size, Proportion, Substance: Dogs 27.5 inches and up at the withers; bitches 25.5 inches and up at the withers. Dogs are approximately 100 pounds and up, bitches approximately 80 pounds and up at maturity, with plenty of bone and substance. While large size is important, type, character,

KOMONDOR

Ch. Kurcafuredi-Subas Edi with owner Maria Aboczky.

Head study of the Komondor. Under the cords is a strong head. The muzzle is slightly shorter than the back skull. Dark pigment for nose, lips and eye rims is very important. Eyes are dark and expressive. Head planes are parallel with a moderate stop. Ears are triangular with medium leather and set below the level of the topskull.

symmetry, movement and ruggedness are of the greatest importance and are on no account to be sacrificed for size alone. The body is slightly longer than the height at the withers. Height below the minimum is a fault.

Head: The head is large. The length of the head from occiput to tip of nose is approximately $2/5$ the height of the dog at the withers. The skin around the eyes and on the muzzle is dark. *Eyes*—Medium-sized and almond-shaped, not too deeply set. The iris of the eye is dark brown. Edges of the eyelids are gray or black. Light eyes are a fault. Blue eyes are a disqualification. *Ears*—In shape the ear is an elongated triangle with a slightly rounded tip. Medium-set and hanging and long enough to reach to the inner corner of the eye on the opposite side of the head. Erect ears or ears that move toward an erect position are a fault. *Skull*—The skull is broad with well-developed arches over the eyes. The occiput is fairly well-developed and the stop is moderate. *Muzzle*—The muzzle is wide, coarse and truncated. Measured from inner corner of the eye to tip of nose the muzzle is $2/5$ of the total length of the head. The top of the muzzle is straight and is parallel to the top of the skull. Underjaw is well-developed and broad. Lips are tight and are black in color. Ideally gums and palate are dark or black. *Nose*—Nose is wide and the front of the nose forms a right angle with the top of the muzzle. The nostrils are wide. The nose is black. A dark gray or dark brown nose is not desirable but is acceptable. A flesh colored nose is a disqualification. *Bite*—Bite is scissors; a level bite is acceptable. A distinctly overshot or undershot bite is a fault. Any missing teeth is a serious fault. Three or more missing teeth is a disqualification.

Breed Standard

Neck: Muscular, of medium length, moderately arched, with no dewlap. The head erect.

Topline: The back is level and strong.

Body: Characterized by a powerful, deep chest, which is muscular and proportionately wide. The breast is broad and well muscled. The belly is somewhat drawn up at the rear. The rump is wide, muscular and slopes slightly towards the root of the tail. Softness or lack of good muscle tone is a fault.

A beautiful Komondor head. This is Duna at three years of age.

Tail: A continuation of the rump line, hanging and long enough to reach the hocks.
   Slightly curved upwards and/or to one side at its end. Even when the dog is moving or excited, the greater part of the tail is raised no higher than the level of the back. A short or curly tail is a fault.

Forequarters: Shoulders are well laid back. Forelegs straight, well-boned and muscular. Viewed from any side, the legs are like vertical columns. The upper arms are carried close to the body, without loose elbows.

Feet: Strong, rather large and with close, well-arched toes. Pads are hard, elastic and black or gray. Ideally, nails are black or gray, although light nails are acceptable.

Hindquarters: The steely, strong bone structure is covered with highly-developed muscles. The

KOMONDOR

A famous Hungarian sire: Int. Ch. Ohegyi Aladar, owned by Ferenc Lehoczky.

legs are straight as viewed from the rear. Stifles are well-bent. Rear dewclaws must be removed.

Coat: Characteristic of the breed is the dense, protective coat. The puppy coat is relatively soft, but it shows a tendency to fall into cord-like curls. The young adult coat, or intermediate coat, consists of very short cords next to the skin which may be obscured by the sometimes lumpy looking fluff on the outer ends of the cords. The mature coat consists of a dense, soft, woolly undercoat much like the puppy coat, and a coarser outer coat that is wavy or curly. The coarser hairs of the outer coat trap the softer undercoat, forming permanent, strong cords that are felt-like to the touch. A grown dog is entirely covered with a heavy coat of these tassel-like cords, which form naturally. It must be remembered that the length of the Komondor's coat is a function of age, and a younger dog must never be penalized for having a shorter coat. Straight or silky coat is a fault. Failure of the coat to cord by two years of age is a disqualification. Short, smooth coat on both head and legs is a disqualification.

Color: Color of the coat is white, but not always the pure white of a brushed coat. A small amount of cream or buff shading is some-

Breed Standard

> **THE BIGGER THE BETTER: A QUESTION OF SIZE**
>
> The Hungarian standards through the ages have asked for a large dog. The original AKC standard (1937) said, "The bigger the better." Hungarian dogs in general were larger, broader and more substantial than dogs bred in the US. The size difference has increased in the last few years with many dogs in the US not only smaller but narrower and lighter boned. Although there is a lower limit for both sexes, there are many champions under those limits, as American judges pay little attention to size below the limit. I for one deplore what seems to be the making of an American dog that the Hungarians would not like at all. No one wants a big dog that is not sound, but we also do not want a dog that the Hungarians would not even recognize. Periodically American breeders ask for an upper size limit. I just hope this is not allowed in my lifetime.

times seen in puppies, but fades with maturity. In the ideal specimen the skin is gray. Pink skin is not desirable but is acceptable. Color other than white, with the exception of small amounts of cream or buff in puppies, is a disqualification.

Gait: Light, leisurely and balanced. The Komondor takes long strides, is very agile and light on his feet. The head is carried slightly forward when the dog trots.

The foregoing is a description of the ideal Komondor. Any deviation should be penalized in direct proportion to the extent of that deviation. Extreme deviation in any part should be penalized to the extent that the dog is effectively eliminated from competition.

Disqualifications:
Blue eyes.
Flesh-colored nose.
Three or more missing teeth.
Failure of the coat to cord by two years of age.
Short, smooth coat on both head and legs.
Color other than white, with the exception of small amounts of cream or buff in puppies.

Approved June 14, 1994
Effective July 31, 1994

The Komondor's light and balanced gait in the show ring attests to its correct structure and overall soundness. Int. Ch. Jászkisére Kócos Csupar and owner/handler Gábor Korózs.

KOMONDOR

An attractive young Kom before the cords have been fully developed.

THE FCI STANDARD FOR THE KOMONDOR

The translation from Hungarian by Joy C. Levy, with help from Dr. George Halasi-Kun and Maria Zankowich.

EFFECTIVE ORIGINAL STANDARD PUBLICATION DATE
January 1, 2000

ORIGIN
Hungary

USE
Shepherd Dog

FCI CLASSIFICATION
Breed Group I: Guarding and Herding Dogs (excepting the Swiss Alps Dogs). Section 1: Shepherd Dogs. Without working test.

SHORT HISTORICAL REVIEW
It is an ancient Hungarian shepherd breed of Asiatic origin. The ancient version in all probability arrived in the Karpathian Basin with the ancient migrating shepherding Hungarians.

GENERAL APPEARANCE
Large-bodied and strongly constructed. Its unique appearance and dignified behavior arouse respect, admiration and perhaps even some fear in the observer. By nature it is reserved. The whole robust body is covered with shaggy, thick, long hair, inclined to get felty.

In the side view, the truck and limbs diverge only to a slight degree from square; they show a rectangular form, longer than it is high. The head is thickly haired and rises above the plane of the back. The tail hangs down and curves almost to horizontal at the end. The color of the hair is bone-white.

BEHAVIOR AND CHARACTER
In protecting and guarding livestock, property and house, he displays unshakable courage. Without a sound, he attacks boldly. Because of that, he considers the area protected by him as his own and does not allow any strange creature to set foot on it. He is by nature mistrustful. By day he willingly lies around so that he can oversee his area. At night he moves around continuously.

HEAD
The head is broad, in proportion to the body. Not even the thick

Breed Standard

> **IMPORTANT MEASUREMENTS**
> Trunk/Height at Withers: = 104% often 100–108%
> Depth of Chest/Height at Withers: = 45% often 50–56%
> Width of Chest/Height at Withers: = 28% often 30%
> Measurement on the Girdle[1] /Height at Withers: = 116% often 120%
> Length of Head[2]/Height at Withers: = 41%
> Length of Muzzle[3]/Length of Head: = 42%
> Length of Ear/Length of Head: = 60%
>
> [1] The girdle is measured with a tape just behind the elbows in a vertical plane. It is slightly behind the highest point of the withers.
> [2] Nose-mirror to occiput—the nose-mirror is the front (vertical) plane of the nose, where a nose-print is taken.
> [3] Stop to nose-mirror.

umbrella-like hair makes it seem disproportionate.

BRAIN CASE
Skull: Domed. The brows are well-developed.
Stop: Fairly perseptible, but not too steep.

FACIAL PART OF THE SKULL
Nose-mirror: Cut at a right angle and black.
Muzzle: Not pointed. The ridge of the nose is straight.
Lips: Black, fitting tight to the teeth, the corners fringed.
Jaws/Teeth: The jaw is richly muscled, strong and large. Regular formula full scissors bite is required.
Jowls: Broad and medium long.
Eyes: Straight, not slanted, dark brown in color. The black eyerims fit the eyeballs tightly.
Ears: Set medium high on the domed crown of the head, definitely hanging, V- or U- shaped. They do not move upwards either in watching or attacking.

NECK
Really well-muscled. The neck makes an angle of 35° with the horizontal. At rest it is almost a continuation of the topline. It is short rather than medium long. There is no dewlap nor is there a ruff.

BODY
Topline: The body parts creating the topline are wide and richly muscled.
Withers: Long enough, higher in front.
Back: Short.
Loin: Medium long.
Croup: Wide, medium long, mildly sloping.
Chest: Broad and strongly muscled, medium deep, wide, long.
Belly: A little tucked up.

The adult Komondor's coat should be longest on the rear regions.

TAIL
Set low, definitely hanging. The end shows a slight curve approaching the horizontal. In a state of excitement it is lifted no higher than the topline. It is desirable for the tail to reach to the hock.

LIMBS
Front Legs: The shaggy hair of the legs to a great degree hinder an evaluation of the limbs. The front legs are like columns, parallel; looking from the front and the side, they are vertical. The chest is wide, which results in wide and thick freely moving limbs. The limbs are closely attached to the body. The skeleton is strong and massive. The joints are large.
Shoulders: The shoulder blade is a little steep. The points of the shoulder and the breast bone are in the same vertical plane.
Paws: Large, closed, with toes tightly adjacent to each other. The soles are slate-gray, full and elastic. The nails are gray.

Rear legs: The back legs support the trunk with relatively steep angulation. It is desirable for the medium croup to continue into broad, muscular and full limbs.
Thighs: Powerfully muscled, bulky.
Paws: The rear paws are longer than the front ones; otherwise they are identical. Dewclaws should be removed.

MOVEMENT
Motion is light, easy and dignified. The stride is elongated, covering a lot of ground.

SKIN
The skin contains much pigment and is slate-gray in color. It is advantageous for the gums and the roof of the mouth to also be darkly pigmented. Partially pigmented and pink-skinned individuals are not desirable.

HAIR
The whole body is covered with long hair. The coat consists of rougher guard hairs and finer fluff underfur. The proportion of outer hair to fluff determines the type of coat.

The basic requirement is shaggy hair, tending to felting. There occurs a hair type of corded character having dense waves; the rather tiny curls of these cords do not get felty at all, or at least to a much lesser extent.

Breed Standard

The length of the hair is greatest on the hindquarters, the loin and the region of the thigh (at least 20–27 cm). It is medium long on the back, the sides of the chest, over the shoulders (at least 15–22 cm) and shorter on the jowls, the brows, the crown of the head, the ears, the neck and the legs (10–18 cm). It is shortest on the lips and the lower part of the legs (9–11 cm).

A combed-out coat and an entirely ungroomed coat are not desirable.

The color is bone-white.

SIZE AND WEIGHT
Dogs: At least 70 cm (27 in) 50–60 kg (110–132 lbs).
Bitches: At least 65 cm (25 in) 40–50 kg (88–110 lbs).

FAULTS
Considering all deviation from the above mentioned point faults, the classification must stand in proportion to the degree of deviation.

The species shows few type faults; to a great extent it is uniform, because from the beginning it has been bred with identical breeding goals.

- Deficient pigmentation on the nose-mirror, the eyelids and the edge of the eyelids
- Missing teeth, misaligned incisors
- Loose eyelids
- Loose shoulders
- Loose, soft paws
- Cowhocks
- Curled tail
- Insufficient size

DISQUALIFYING FAULTS
- Weak, poorly muscled body construction
- Entropion, ectropion
- Overbite, underbite, crossbite
- Erect, flying ears
- Short tail 3 cm (1 in above the hock)
- Heavy limbs and movement faults
- Colored or pied hair
- Smaller measurements than the standard's lower limits

POSTSCRIPT
Dogs must possess two normally developed testicles visible to the eye, seated entirely in the scrotum.

This standard was published on the Hungarian Kennel Club website, at www.meoe.net.

Breeder Joszef Bukovski and two of his Karcagpusztai Komondors.

YOUR PUPPY

KOMONDOR

CHOOSING A BREEDER AND PUPPY

Before you begin your search for a Komondor breeder and puppy, be sure that the Komondor is absolutely the breed for you. There are many breeds that are much easier to obtain and keep. You should read everything you can find before you think of getting this breed. The place to start is to contact both the Komondor Club of America and the Middle Atlantic States Komondor Club. Both clubs can provide information and lists of reputable breeders. Under no circumstances should you consider getting a Komondor puppy from a source other than a reputable breeder. The temperament of the Komondor is such that how a pup is raised from birth makes a big difference in his development. It would be nice to visit a few breeders and meet their dogs, but there are not too many Komondors or Komondor breeders in the country. Some get their original stock from Hungary, and breeders often have to mate their dogs with Komondors from quite far away. You should be able to meet at least one parent of a puppy that you are considering.

Both clubs feel that you should buy from breeders who have the

> **NAMING KOMONDORS**
> The Hungarians often name their kennels for the towns in which they reside. Szentivani, for example, means from Saint Ivan, a town near Budapest. The author's kennel name, Hercegvaros, means Princeton, the New Jersey town that is the home of one of the world's top universities. All puppies in the breeder's first litter have names beginning with B, and so forth. Many breeders follow this pattern and it makes keeping track of dogs and litters very simple! The author is still waiting to breed her Hercegvaros Zorro!

Rely upon the breeder's discretion when selecting the Kom puppy best for your living situation.

hips of their breeding stock x-rayed and the x-rays sent to the Orthopedic Foundation for Animals (OFA). This organization will certify dogs that are free from hip dysplasia (HD). This is important for any large breed. Komondors have less HD than many large breeds, but it does occur in the breed and it can be debilitating. It will be difficult to check the HD status if you get dogs from abroad. No one can guarantee that a young puppy will not develop HD, but the chances for good hips are vastly better if both parents are certified. Good breeders will give some guarantee about health in general and hip dysplasia in particular.

As for choosing an individual puppy, I have had the best luck when a breeder in whom I have confidence picks out a puppy for me if I cannot see the litter. Likewise, a good breeder will assist you in choosing a pup out of a litter that you visit. It is wise to tell the breeder what you are looking for: do you want a working dog, a

A young Komondor should appear bright, alert and inquisitive.

Don't choose on cuteness alone. Choose an active and alert puppy who is interested in getting to know you.

SELECTING FROM THE LITTER

Before you visit a litter of puppies, promise yourself that you won't fall for the first pretty face you see! Decide on your goals for your puppy—show prospect, guardian, obedience competitor, family companion—and then look for a puppy who displays the appropriate qualities. In most litters, there is an alpha pup (the bossy puppy), and occasionally a shy fellow who is less confident, with the rest of the litter falling somewhere in the middle. "Middle-of-the-roaders" are safe bets for most families and novice competitors.

48 KOMONDOR

Two nice youngsters bred by Gail and Gordon Sheddy.

Adult and puppy, Ch. Szentivani Ingo and Ch. Borsodi Gangos.

house guard, a show dog, etc.? What points are important to you? Do you want a Komondor on the larger or smaller end of the size spectrum? Remember that having a 31-inch male is rather like living with a Shetland pony! Do you care about pigment, eye color, etc., or is your main interest stable temperament? A good breeder will have some idea as to which puppy in a litter is more gentle and which is more aggressive. Good breeders know each puppy in a litter and have an idea of how they will mature. If you visit a litter with the intent of picking a puppy, it may be impossible to do so in just one encounter. If a puppy has just eaten and wants to sleep, he may appear too lethargic, but after a good sleep he may be too active for your taste.

The best advice is to choose your breeder with care. From picking the pup to raising and caring for him, with any Komondor you are likely to need a lot of help from the breeder. Komondors are very likely to act very differently from any other dogs you have have owned or met, and you will likely continue seeking advice from the breeder as the puppy grows up. I would never buy a dog from a breeder I did not like and trust. Most Komondor breeders will insist that if you find you cannot keep the dog, you will return the dog to them for rehoming.

In no case should you buy a Komondor with the intent of making money by breeding the dog. Not only is this not something to be attempted by a novice but it also is not a money-making venture. The most experienced breeders have all encountered breeding problems. If a breeder does not lose too much money on a litter, it's considered fortunate!

A COMMITTED NEW OWNER
By now you should understand what makes the Komondor a most unique and special dog, one that you feel will fit nicely into your family and lifestyle. If you have researched breeders, you should be able to recognize a knowledgeable and responsible Komondor breeder who cares not only about his pups but also about what kind of owner you will be. If you have completed the final step in your new journey, you have found a litter, or possibly two, of quality Komondor pups.

A visit with the puppies and their breeder should be an education in itself. Breed research, breeder selection and puppy visitation are very important aspects of finding the puppy of your dreams. Beyond that, these things also lay the foundation for a successful future with your pup. Puppy personalities within each litter vary, from the easygoing puppy to the one who is dominant and assertive, with most pups falling somewhere in between. By spending time with the puppies you will be able to recognize certain behaviors and what these behaviors indicate about each pup's temperament. Which type of pup will complement your family dynamics is best determined by observing the puppies in action within their "pack." Your breeder's expertise and recommendations are so valuable. Although you may fall in love with a bold and brassy male, the breeder may suggest that another pup would be best for you. The breeder's experience in rearing Komondor pups and matching

Meeting the litter can be very exciting if not a bit overwhelming. Prepare yourself with a list of questions for the breeder before arriving at the kennel. Breeders, Gail and Gordon Sheddy.

Though these Kom puppies look content on the stone steps, you must provide your puppy with a cozy bed to call his own.

their temperaments with appropriate humans offers the best assurance that your pup will meet your needs and expectations. The type of puppy that you select is just as important as your decision that the Komondor is the breed for you.

The decision to live with a Komondor is a serious commitment and not one to be taken lightly. The Komondor needs an owner who understands the breed and is prepared to deal with his unique outlook on life. Further, this puppy is a living sentient being that will be dependent on you for basic survival for his entire life. Beyond the basics of survival—food, water, shelter and protection—he needs much, much more. The new pup needs love, nurturing and a proper canine education to mold him into a responsible, well-behaved canine citizen. Your Komondor's health and good manners will need consistent monitoring and regular "tune-ups," so your job as a responsible dog owner will be ongoing throughout every stage of his life. If you are not prepared to accept these responsibilities and commit to them for at least the next decade, likely longer, then you are not prepared to own a dog of any breed.

Although the responsibilities of owning a dog may at times tax your patience, the joy of living with your Komondor far outweighs the workload, and a well-mannered adult dog is worth your time and effort. Before your very eyes, your new charge will grow up to be your most loyal friend, devoted to you unconditionally.

YOUR KOMONDOR SHOPPING LIST

Just as expectant parents prepare a nursery for their baby, so should you ready your home for the arrival of your Komondor pup. If you have the necessary puppy supplies purchased and in place before he comes home, it

CRATE EXPECTATIONS

To make the crate more inviting to your puppy, you can offer his first meal or two inside the crate, always keeping the crate door open so that he does not feel confined. Keep a favorite toy or two in the crate for him to play with while inside. You can also cover the crate at night with a lightweight sheet to make it more den-like and remove the stimuli of household activity. Never put him into his crate as punishment or as you are scolding him, since he will then associate his crate with negative situations and avoid going there.

Your Puppy

will ease the puppy's transition from the warmth and familiarity of his mom and littermates to the brand-new environment of his new home and human family. You will be too busy to stock up and prepare your house after your pup comes home, that's for sure! Imagine how a pup must feel upon being transported to a strange new place. It's up to you to comfort him and to let your little pup know that he is going to be happy with you.

Food and Water Bowls
We strongly recommend stainless steel or pottery bowls. Some owners have reported fading noses with plastic bowls. We elevate bowls (most will sit nicely in a small bucket) because the dogs have somewhat cleaner mouths when they eat from raised bowls. Some Komondors routinely eat lying down and will knock bowls and food onto the ground. You will have to decide about this. We give water in containers that are elevated off the ground with openings that do not allow the dog to get his whole head in the water. This saves much dripping on the floor.

The Dog Crate
If you think that crates are tools of punishment and confinement for when a dog has misbehaved, think again. Most breeders and almost all trainers recommend a crate as the preferred house-training aid as well as for all-around puppy training and safety. Because dogs are natural den creatures that prefer cave-like environments, the benefits of crate use are many. The crate provides the puppy with his very own "safe house," a cozy place to sleep, take a break or seek comfort with a favorite toy; a travel aid to house your dog when on the road, at motels or at the vet's office; a training aid to help teach your

Protective breeds like the Komondor require a large wire crate so that the dog gets a full view of what is going on around him.

COST OF OWNERSHIP
The purchase price of your puppy is merely the first expense in the typical dog budget. Quality dog food, veterinary care (sickness and health maintenance), dog supplies and grooming costs will add up to big bucks every year. Can you adequately afford to support a canine addition to the family?

An adult Komondor will take up most of his crate, so it is wise to get the biggest one available.

puppy proper toileting habits; and a place of solitude when non-dog people happen to drop by and don't want a lively puppy—or even a well-behaved adult dog—saying hello or begging for attention.

Crates come in several types, although the wire crate and the fiberglass airline-type crate are the most popular. Both are safe and your puppy will adjust to either one, so the choice is up to you. The wire crates offer better visibility for the pup as well as better ventilation. Many of the wire crates easily collapse into suitcase-size carriers. The fiberglass crates, similar to those used by the airlines for animal transport, are sturdier and more den-like. However, the fiberglass crates do not collapse and are less ventilated than a wire crate, which can be problematic in hot weather. Some of the newer crates are made of heavy plastic mesh; they are very lightweight and fold up into slim-line suitcases. However, a mesh crate might not be suitable for a pup with manic chewing habits or a large adult.

Don't bother with a puppy-sized crate. Although your Komondor will be a little fellow when you bring him home, he will grow up in the blink of an eye and your puppy crate will be useless. Purchase a crate that will accommodate an adult Komondor. He can stand upward of 27.5 inches when full-grown, so purchase an extra-large crate with dimensions that will allow him to fully stand up, lie down and turn around. For house-training and to create a cozy space for the pup

Your Puppy

where he won't feel lost in a too-big crate, removable divider panels can be used to partition the crate.

BEDDING AND CRATE PADS

Your puppy will enjoy some type of soft bedding in his "room" (the crate), something he can snuggle into to feel cozy and secure. Old towels or blankets are good choices for a young pup, since he may (and probably will) have a toileting accident or two in the crate or decide to chew on the bedding material. Once he is fully trained and out of the early chewing stage, you can replace the puppy bedding with a permanent crate pad if you prefer. Crate pads and other dog beds run the gamut from inexpensive to high-end doggie-designer styles, but don't splurge on the good stuff until you are sure that your puppy is reliable and won't tear it up or make a mess on it.

PUPPY TOYS

A fun array of safe doggie toys will help satisfy your puppy's chewing instincts and distract him from gnawing on the leg of your antique chair or your new leather sofa. Most puppy toys are cute and look as if they would be a lot of fun, but not all are necessarily safe or good for your puppy, so use caution when you go puppy-toy shopping.

Komondor puppies are playful and do enjoy toys. They are not retrievers, so they will rarely bring you back a ball or a stick. Their

TOYS 'R SAFE

The vast array of tantalizing puppy toys is staggering. Stroll through any pet shop or pet-supply outlet and you will see that the choices can be overwhelming. However, not all dog toys are safe or sensible. Most very young puppies enjoy soft woolly toys that they can snuggle with and carry around. (You know they have outgrown them when they shred them up!) Avoid toys that have buttons, tabs or other enhancements that can be chewed off and swallowed. Soft toys that squeak are fun, but make sure your puppy does not disembowel the toy and remove (and swallow) the squeaker. Toys that rattle or make noise can excite a puppy, but they present the same danger as the squeaky kind and so require supervision. Hard rubber toys that bounce can also entertain a pup, but make sure that the toy is too big for your pup to swallow.

Komondor puppies are curious creatures and must have access only to areas that you deem safe and secure, both indoors and out.

usual approach to such things is to watch you throw something and remain where they are as if to say, "That was nice. Now go get it." They love to chew on sticks they find in the yard, and this does not seem to hurt them. They like balls that they can pick up or large ones that they can push around. Sterile bones or stuffed bones are also enjoyed, but be careful that they do not splinter or break into small pieces, as this is dangerous. Most Komondors adore Greenies®, which they devour; they do seem to help clean teeth too. We do not recommend rawhides. Not only do rawhides stain paws and mouths, but Koms treat rawhides like food and will not share with other dogs. Rawhides also can be dangerous. Pieces of rawhide are easily swallowed after they get soft and gummy from chewing, and dogs have been known to choke on pieces of ingested rawhide.

Nylon and hard rubber bones are safe to gnaw on and come in sizes appropriate for all age groups and breeds. Soft woolly toys are Komondor puppy favorites. They come in a wide variety of cute shapes and sizes; some look like little stuffed animals. Some even talk! Puppies love to shake them up and toss them about or simply carry them around. Be careful of fuzzy toys that have button eyes or noses that your pup could chew off and swallow, and make sure that he does not disembowel a talking toy or squeaky toy to remove the mechanism inside. Braided rope toys are similar in that they are fun to chew and toss around, but they shred easily and the strings are easy to swallow. The strings are not digestible and, if the puppy doesn't pass them in his stool, he could end up at the vet's office. Your puppy should be closely monitored with rope toys.

If you believe that your pup has ingested a piece of one of his toys, check his stool for the next couple of days to see if he passes the item when he defecates. At the same time, also watch for signs of intestinal distress. A call to your veterinarian might be in order to get his advice and be on the safe side.

An all-time favorite toy for puppies (young and old!) is the empty gallon milk jug. Hard plastic juice containers—46 ounces or more—are also excellent. Such containers make lots of noise when they are batted about, and puppies go crazy with delight as they play with them. However, they don't often last very long, so be sure to remove and replace them when they get chewed up.

A word of caution about homemade toys: be careful with your choices of non-traditional play objects. Never use old shoes or socks, since a puppy cannot distinguish between the old ones on which he's allowed to chew and the new ones in your closet that are strictly off limits. That principle applies to anything that resembles something that you don't want your puppy to chew.

COLLARS AND LEASHES

A lightweight nylon collar is the best choice for a very young pup. Quick-click collars are easy to put on and remove, and they can be adjusted as the puppy grows. Introduce him to his collar as soon as he comes home to get him accustomed to wearing it. He'll get used to it quickly and won't mind a bit. Make sure that it is snug enough that it won't slip off, yet loose enough to be comfortable for the pup. You should be able to slip two fingers between the collar and his neck. Check the collar often, as puppies grow in spurts, and his collar can become too tight almost overnight.

For the adult, we recommend choke collars with long links to leave on the dog for most purposes. For sharp obedience work, you may prefer the standard choke collars, but if these are left on the dog they are likely to wear down the coat more than the long-link collars do. Halti collars or head collars are also preferred by many. For difficult dogs, some people use prong collars, especially for training in crowded places. We find that adding extra links to the lightest-weight prong collars works better than using the heaviest-weight links. For showing, either lightweight martingale collars (metal preferred) or standard nylon show collars and leads are most popular.

We use 6-foot leather latigo leads; either $1/2$ inch- or $5/8$ inch-wide ones are most comfortable. For initial puppy walks and house-training purposes, you should invest in a shorter lead so that you have more control over the puppy.

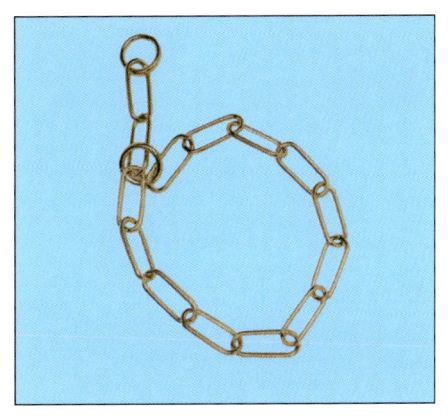

A fur-saver choke collar with longer links is the best choice for the Komondor.

56   KOMONDOR

Your puppy's world presents many exciting challenges and new experiences. It is up to you to provide him with a safe and comfortable environment.

At first, you don't want him wandering too far away from you, and when taking him out for toileting you will want to keep him in the specific area chosen for his potty spot.

For the leash-trained Komondor, many people have very good luck with retractable leads. I always keep short traffic leads, 2 feet in length or, for tall dogs, just a traffic handle to use when I take a Komondor anywhere where he must be in close quarters with people or other dogs.

Dogs investigate with their mouths and Koms seem particularly to like sticks. Always keep an eye on anything your dog is chewing to ensure his safety.

HOME SAFETY FOR YOUR PUPPY

The importance of puppy-proofing cannot be overstated. In addition to making your house comfortable for your Komondor's arrival, you also must make sure that your house is safe for your puppy before you bring him home. There are countless hazards in the owner's personal living environment that a pup can sniff, chew, swallow or destroy. Many are obvious; others are not. Do a thorough advance house check to remove or rearrange those things that could hurt your puppy, keeping any potentially dangerous items out of areas to which he will have access.

Electrical cords are especially dangerous, since puppies view them as irresistible chew toys. Unplug and remove all exposed cords or fasten them beneath baseboards where the puppy cannot reach them. Veterinarians and firefighters can tell you horror stories about electrical burns and house fires that resulted from puppy-chewed electrical cords. Consider this a most serious precaution for your puppy and the rest of your family.

Scout your home for tiny objects that might be seen at a pup's eye level. Keep medication bottles and cleaning supplies well out of reach, and do the same with waste baskets and other trash containers. It goes without saying that you should not use rodent poison or other toxic chemicals in any puppy area and that you must keep such containers safely locked up. You will be amazed at how many places a curious puppy can discover!

Once your house has cleared inspection, check your yard. A sturdy fence, well embedded into the ground, will give your dog a safe place to play and potty. Komondors are large dogs, so a 6-foot-high fence is necessary to contain an agile youngster or adult. Check the fence periodically for necessary repairs. If there is a weak link or space to squeeze through, you can be sure a determined Komondor will discover it.

The garage and shed can be hazardous places for a pup, as things like fertilizers, chemicals and tools are usually kept there. It's best to keep these areas off limits to the pup. Antifreeze is especially dangerous to dogs, as they find the taste appealing and it takes only a few licks from the driveway to kill a dog, puppy or adult, small breed or large.

VISITING THE VETERINARIAN
A good veterinarian who is willing to work with your dog and his breed-specific concerns is your Komondor puppy's best health-insurance policy. If you do not already have a vet, ask your breeder and other experienced Komondor people for recommendations in your area so that you can select a vet before you bring your Komondor puppy home. Also arrange for your puppy's first veterinary examination beforehand, since many vets do not have appointments available immediately, and your puppy should visit the vet within a day or so of coming home.

It's important to make sure your puppy's first visit to the vet is a pleasant and positive one. The vet should take great care to befriend the pup and handle him gently to make their first meeting a positive experience. The vet will give the pup a thorough physical examination and set up a schedule for vaccinations and other necessary wellness visits. Be sure to show your vet any health and inoculation records, which you should have received from your breeder. Your vet is a great source of canine health information, so

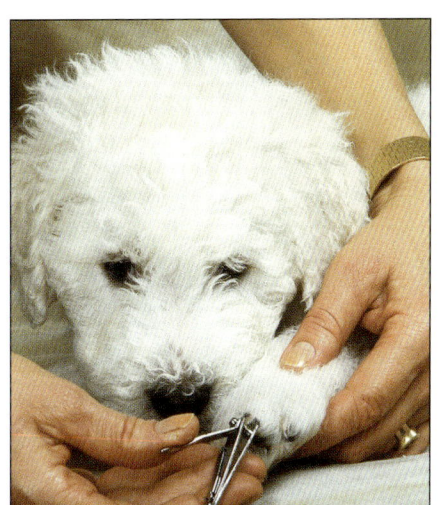

A human nail clipper suffices for a young puppy, but a nail clipper made for canines is needed for an older dog.

A comfy couch, a chew toy and a friend—these Kom pups seem right at home.

be sure to ask questions and take notes. Creating a health journal for your puppy will make a handy reference for his wellness and any future health problems that may arise.

MEETING THE FAMILY
Your Komondor's homecoming is an exciting time for all members of the family, and it's only natural that everyone will be eager to meet him, pet him and play with him. However, for the puppy's sake, it's best to make these initial family meetings as uneventful as possible so that the pup is not overwhelmed with too much too soon. Remember, he has just left his dam and his littermates and is away from the breeder's home for the first time. Despite his fuzzy wagging tail, he is still apprehensive and wondering where he is and who all these strange humans are. It's best to let him explore on his own and meet the family members as he feels comfortable. Let him investigate all the new smells, sights and sounds at his own pace. Children should be especially careful to not get overly excited, use loud voices or hug the pup too tightly. Be calm, gentle and affectionate, and be ready to comfort him if he appears frightened or uneasy.

Be sure to show your puppy his new crate during this first day home. Toss a treat or two inside the crate; if he associates the crate with food, he will associate the crate with good things. If he is comfortable with the crate, you can offer him his first meal inside it. Leave the door ajar so he can wander in and out as he chooses.

FIRST NIGHT IN HIS NEW HOME
So much has happened in your Komondor puppy's first day away from the breeder. He's had his first car ride to his new home. He's met his new human family and perhaps the other family pets. He has explored his new house and yard, at least those places where he is to be allowed during his first weeks at home. He may have visited his new veterinarian. He has eaten his first meal or two away from his dam and littermates. Surely that's enough to tire out an eight-week-old Komondor pup—or so you hope!

It's bedtime. During the day, the pup investigated his crate, which is his new den and sleeping space, so it is not entirely strange to him. Line the crate with a soft towel or blanket that he can snuggle into and gently place him into the crate for the night. Some breeders send home a piece of bedding from where the pup slept with his littermates, and those familiar scents are a great comfort for the puppy on his first night without his siblings.

He will probably whine or cry. The puppy is objecting to the confinement and the fact that he is alone for the first time. This can be a stressful time for you as well as for the pup. It's important that you remain strong and don't let the puppy out of his crate to comfort him. He will fall asleep eventually. If you release him, the puppy will learn that crying means "out" and will continue that habit. You are laying the groundwork for future habits. Some breeders find that soft music can soothe a crying pup and help him get to sleep.

SOCIALIZING YOUR PUPPY
The first 20 weeks of your Komondor puppy's life are the most important of his entire lifetime. A properly socialized puppy will grow up to be a

Early socialization and interaction with his littermates is a good head start in life for any puppy. You also can learn a great deal from watching the littermates play with one another.

KOMONDOR

Komondors do a lot of growing in their first six months. This puppy is bigger than the adults of many breeds!

confident and stable adult who will be a pleasure to live with and a welcome addition to the neighborhood.

The importance of socialization cannot be overemphasized. Research on canine behavior has proven that puppies who are not exposed to new sights, sounds, people and animals during their first 20 weeks of life will grow up to be timid and fearful, even aggressive, and unable to flourish outside of their home environment.

Socializing your puppy is not difficult and, in fact, will be a fun time for you both. Lead training goes hand in hand with socialization, so your puppy will be learning how to walk on a lead at the same time that he's meeting the neighborhood. Because the Komondor is such a fascinating breed, everyone will enjoy meeting "the new kid on the block." Take him for short walks to the park and to other dog-friendly places where he will encounter new people, especially children. Puppies automatically recognize children as "little people" and are drawn to play with them. Just make sure that you supervise these meetings and that the children do not get too rough or encourage him to play too hard. An overzealous pup can often nip too hard, frightening the child and in turn making the puppy overly excited. A bad experience in puppyhood can

Your Puppy

impact a dog for life, so a pup that has a negative experience with a child may grow up to be shy or even aggressive around children.

Take your puppy along on your daily errands. Puppies are natural "people magnets," and most people who see your pup will want to pet him. All of these encounters will help to mold him into a confident adult dog. Likewise, you will soon feel like a confident, responsible dog owner, rightly proud of your handsome Komondor.

Be especially careful of your puppy's encounters and experiences during the eight-to-ten-week-old period, which is also called the "fear period." This is a serious imprinting period, and all contact during this time should be gentle and positive. A frightening or negative event could leave a permanent impression that could affect his future behavior if a similar situation arises.

Also make sure that your puppy has received his first and second rounds of vaccinations before you expose him to other dogs or bring him to places that other dogs may frequent. Avoid dog parks and other strange-dog areas until your vet assures you that your puppy is fully immunized and resistant to the diseases that can be passed between canines. Discuss safe early socialization with your breeder, as some breeders recommend socializing the puppy even before he has received all of his inoculations.

LEADER OF THE PUPPY'S PACK

Like other canines, your puppy needs an authority figure, someone he can look up to and regard as the leader of his "pack." His first pack leader was his dam, who taught him to be polite and not chew too hard on her ears or nip at her muzzle. He learned those same lessons from his littermates. If he played too rough, they cried in pain and stopped the game, which sent an important message to the rowdy puppy.

As puppies play together, they are also struggling to determine who will be the boss. Being pack animals, dogs need someone to be in charge. If a litter of puppies remained together beyond puppyhood, one of the pups would emerge as the strongest one, the one who calls the shots.

Once your puppy leaves the pack, he will look intuitively for a new leader. If he does not

Here's a dynamic trio with their dam, their first and fearless pack leader.

recognize you as that leader, he will try to assume that position for himself. Of course, it is hard to imagine your adorable Komondor puppy trying to be in charge when he is so small and seemingly helpless. You must remember that these are natural canine instincts. Do not cave in and allow your pup to get the upper "paw"!

Just as socialization is so important during these first 20 weeks, so too is your puppy's early education. He was born without any bad habits. He does not know what is good or bad behavior. If he does things like nipping and digging, it's because he is having fun and doesn't know that humans consider these things as "bad." It's your job to teach him proper puppy manners, and this is the best time to accomplish that—before he has developed bad habits, since it is much more difficult to "unlearn" or correct unacceptable learned behavior than to teach good behavior from the start.

A Komondor will guard and protect anything he deems part of his herd—even the pet bird.

> **THE CRITICAL SOCIALIZATION PERIOD**
> Canine research has shown that a puppy's 8th through 16th week is the most critical learning period of his life. This is when the puppy "learns to learn," a time when he needs positive experiences to build confidence and stability. Puppies who are not exposed to different people and situations outside the home during this period can grow up to be fearful and sometimes aggressive. This is also the best time for puppy lessons, since he has not yet acquired any bad habits that could undermine his ability to learn.

Make sure that all members of the family understand the importance of being consistent when training their new puppy. If you tell the puppy to stay off the sofa and your daughter allows him to cuddle on the couch to watch her favorite television show, your pup will be confused about what he is and is not allowed to do. Have a family conference before your pup comes home so that everyone understands the basic principles of puppy training and the rules you have set forth for the pup, and agrees to follow them.

The old saying that "an ounce of prevention is worth a pound of cure" is especially true when it comes to puppies. It is much easier

Your Puppy

to prevent inappropriate behavior than it is to change it. It's also easier and less stressful for the pup, since it will keep discipline to a minimum and create a more positive learning environment for him. That, in turn, will also be easier on you.

Here are a few commonsense tips to keep your belongings safe and your puppy out of trouble:

- Keep your closet doors closed and your shoes, socks and other apparel off the floor so your puppy can't get to them.
- Keep a secure lid on the trash container or put the trash where your puppy can't dig into it. He can't damage what he can't reach!
- Supervise your puppy at all times to make sure he is not getting into mischief. If he starts to chew the corner of the rug, you can distract him instantly by tossing a toy for him to fetch. You also will be able to whisk him outside when you notice that he is about to piddle on the carpet. If you can't see your puppy, you can't teach him or correct his behavior.

SOLVING PUPPY PROBLEMS

CHEWING AND NIPPING

Nipping at fingers and toes is normal puppy behavior. Chewing is also the way that puppies investigate their surroundings. However, you will have to teach your puppy

An orally fixated Kom puppy will think just about anything is chew-worthy; keep an eye on what he puts in his mouth.

that chewing anything other than his toys is not acceptable. That won't happen overnight and at times puppy teeth will test your patience. However, if you allow nipping and chewing to continue, just think about the damage that a mature Komondor can do with a full set of adult teeth.

Whenever your puppy nips your hand or fingers, cry out "Ouch!" in a loud voice, which should startle your puppy and stop him from nipping, even if only for a moment. Immediately distract him by offering a small treat or an appropriate toy for him to chew instead (which means having chew toys and puppy treats handy or in your pockets at all times). Praise him when he takes the toy and tell him what a good fellow he is. Praise is just as or even more important in puppy training as discipline and correction.

Puppies also tend to nip at children more often than adults, since they perceive little ones to be more vulnerable and more similar to their littermates. Teach your children appropriate responses to nipping behavior. If they are unable to handle it themselves, you may have to intervene. Puppy nips can be quite painful and a child's frightened reaction will only encourage a puppy to nip harder, which is a natural canine response. As with all other puppy situations, interaction between your Komondor puppy and children should be supervised.

Chewing on objects, not just family members' fingers and ankles, is also normal canine behavior that can be especially tedious (for the owner, not the pup) during the teething period when the puppy's adult teeth are coming in. At this stage, chewing just plain feels good. Furniture legs and cabinet corners are common puppy favorites. Shoes and other personal items also taste pretty good to a pup.

The best solution is, once again, prevention. If you value something, keep it tucked away and out of reach. You can't hide your dining-room table in a closet, but you can try to deflect the chewing by applying a bitter product made just to deter dogs from chewing. This spray-on substance is vile-tasting, although safe for dogs, and most puppies will avoid the forbidden object after one tiny taste. You also can apply the product to your leather leash if the puppy tries to chew on his lead during leash-training sessions.

> **REPEAT YOURSELF**
> Puppies learn best through repetition. Use the same verbal cues and commands when teaching your puppy new behaviors or correcting for misbehaviors. Be consistent, but not monotonous. Puppies get bored just like puppy owners.

Keep a ready supply of safe chews handy to offer your Komondor as a distraction when he starts to chew on something that's a "no-no." Remember, at this tender age he does not yet know what is permitted or forbidden, so you have to be "on call" every minute he's awake and on the prowl.

You may lose a treasure or two during your puppy's growing-up period, and the furniture could sustain a nasty nick or two. These can be trying times, so be prepared for those inevitable accidents and comfort yourself in knowing that this too shall pass.

JUMPING UP

Puppies will be puppies, and puppies jump up—on you, your guests, your counters and your furniture. Just another normal part of growing up, and one you need to meet head-on before it becomes an ingrained habit and you have 100 pounds of Komondor flying at you in an eager greeting.

The key to jump correction is consistency. You cannot correct your Komondor for jumping up on you today, then allow it to happen tomorrow by greeting him with hugs and kisses. As you have learned by now, consistency is critical to all puppy lessons.

For starters, try turning your back as soon as the puppy jumps. Jumping up is a means of gaining your attention, and if the pup can't see your face, he may get discouraged and learn that he loses eye contact with his beloved master when he jumps up.

Leash corrections also work, and most puppies respond well to a leash tug if they jump. Grasp the leash close to the puppy's collar and give a quick tug downward, using the command "Off." Do not use the word "Down," since "Down" is used to teach the puppy to lie down, which is a separate action that he will learn during his education in the basic commands. As soon as the puppy has backed off, tell him to sit and immediately praise him for doing so. This will take many repetitions and won't be accomplished quickly, so don't get discouraged or give up; you must be even more persistent than your puppy.

A second method used for jump correction is the spritzer bottle. Fill a spray bottle with water mixed with a bit of lemon juice or vinegar. As soon as puppy jumps, command him "Off" and spritz him with the water mixture. Of course, that means having the spray bottle handy whenever or wherever jumping usually happens.

Yet another method to discourage jumping is grasping the puppy's paws and holding them gently but firmly until he struggles to get away. Wait a brief moment or two, then release his paws and give him a command to sit. He should eventually learn that jumping gets him into an uncomfortable predicament.

Children are major victims of puppy jumping, since puppies view little people as ready targets for jumping up as well as nipping.

Such a greeting from a Kom can be a bit overwhelming. Given his size and strength, it's best to greet your dog when he's on all fours.

If your children (or their friends) are unable to dispense jump corrections, you will have to intervene and handle it for them.

Important to prevention is also knowing what you should not do. Never kick your Komondor (for any reason, not just for jumping) or knock him in the chest with your knee. That maneuver could actually harm your puppy. Vets can tell you stories about puppies who suffered broken bones after being banged about when they jumped up.

PUPPY WHINING
Puppies often cry and whine, just as infants and little children do. It's their way of telling us that they are lonely or in need of attention. Your puppy will miss his littermates and will feel insecure when he is left alone. You may be out of the house or just in another room, but he will still feel alone. During these times, the puppy's crate should be his personal comfort station, a place all his own where he can feel safe and secure. Once he learns that being alone is okay and not something to be feared, he will settle down without crying or objecting. You might want to leave a radio on while he is crated, as the sound of human voices can be soothing and will give the impression that people are around.

Give your puppy a favorite cuddly toy or chew toy to entertain him whenever he is crated. You will both be happier: the puppy because he is safe in his den and you because he is quiet, safe and not getting into puppy escapades that can wreak havoc in your house or cause him danger.

To make sure that your puppy will always view his crate as a safe and cozy place, never, ever use the crate as punishment. That's the best way to turn the crate into a negative place that the pup will want to avoid. Sure, you can use the crate for your own peace of mind if your puppy is getting into trouble and needs some "time out." Just don't let him know that! Never scold the pup and immediately place him into the crate. Count to ten, give him a couple of hugs and maybe a treat, then scoot him into his crate.

It's also important not to make a big fuss when he is released from the crate. That will make getting

A clever and tall dog like the Komondor can "counter surf" and steal a snack without ever lifting his front paws.

out of the crate more appealing than being in the crate, which is just the opposite of what you are trying to achieve.

COUNTER SURFING
What we like to call "counter surfing" is a normal extension of jumping and usually starts to happen as soon as a puppy realizes that he is big enough to stand on his hind legs and investigate the good stuff on the kitchen counter or the coffee table. Once again, you have to be there to prevent it! As soon as you see your Komondor even start to raise himself up, startle him with a sharp "No!" or "Aaahh, aaahh!" If he succeeds and manages to get one or both paws on the forbidden surface, smack those paws (firmly but gently) and tell him "Off!" As soon as he's back on all four paws, command him to sit and praise at once.

For surf prevention, make sure to keep any tempting treats or edibles out of reach, where your Komondor can't see or smell them. It's the old rule of prevention yet again.

FOOD GUARDING
Some dogs are picky eaters; others seem to inhale their food without chewing it. Occasionally, the true "chow hound" will become protective of his food, which is one dangerous step toward other aggressive behavior. Food guarding is obvious: your puppy will growl, snarl or even attempt to bite you if you approach his food bowl or put your hand into his pan while he's eating.

This behavior is not acceptable and very preventable! If your puppy is an especially voracious eater, sit next to him occasionally while he eats and dangle your fingers in his food bowl. Don't feed him in a corner, where he could feel possessive of his eating space. Rather, place his food bowl in an open area of your kitchen where you are in close proximity. Occasionally remove his food in mid-meal, tell him he's a good boy and return his bowl.

If your pup becomes possessive of his food, look for other signs of future aggression, like guarding his favorite toys or refusing to obey obedience commands that he knows. Consult an obedience trainer for help in reinforcing obedience so your Komondor will fully understand that you are the boss.

> **TASTY LESSONS**
> The best route to teaching a very young puppy is through his tummy. Use tiny bits of soft puppy treats to teach obedience commands like come, sit and down. Don't overdo treats: schooltime is not meant to be mealtime.

PROPER CARE OF YOUR

KOMONDOR

Adding a Komondor to your household means adding a new family member who will need your care each and every day. When your Komondor pup first comes home, you will start a routine with him so that, as he grows up, your dog will have a daily schedule just as you do. The aspects of your dog's daily care will likewise become regular parts of your day, so you'll both have a new schedule. Dogs learn by consistency and thrive on routine: regular times for meals, exercise, grooming and potty trips are just as important for your dog as they are for you! Your dog's schedule will depend much on your family's daily routine, but remember that you now have a new member of the family who is part of your day every day.

FEEDING

Feeding your dog the best diet is based on various factors, including age, activity level, overall condition and size of breed. When you visit the breeder, he will share with you his advice about the proper diet for your dog based on his experience with the breed and the foods with which he has had success. Likewise, your vet will be a helpful source of advice throughout the dog's life and will aid you in planning a diet for optimal health.

FEEDING THE PUPPY
Of course, your pup's very first food will be his dam's milk. There may be special situations in which pups fail to nurse, necessitating that the breeder hand-feed them with a formula, but for the most part pups spend the first weeks of life nursing from their dam. The breeder weans the pups by gradually introducing solid foods

> **VARIETY IS THE SPICE**
> Although dog-food manufacturers contend that dogs don't like variety in their diets, studies show quite the opposite to be true. Dogs would much rather vary their meals than eat the same old chow day in and day out. Dry kibble is no more exciting for a dog than the same bowl of bran flakes would be for you. Fortunately, there are dozens of varieties available on the market, and your dog will likely show preference for certain flavors over others. A word of warning: don't overdo it or you'll develop a fussy eater who only prefers chopped beef fillet and asparagus tips every night.

and decreasing the milk meals. Pups may even start themselves off on the weaning process, albeit inadvertently, if they snatch bites from their mom's food bowl.

By the time the pups are ready for new homes, they are fully weaned and eating a good puppy food. As a new owner, you may be thinking, "Great! The breeder has taken care of the hard part." Not so fast.

A puppy's first year of life is the time when most of his growth and development takes place. This is a delicate time, and diet plays a huge role in proper skeletal and muscular formation. Improper diet and exercise habits can lead to damaging problems that will compromise the dog's health and movement for his entire life. That being said, new owners should not worry needlessly. With the myriad types of food formulated specifically for growing pups of different-sized breeds, dog-food manufacturers have taken much of the guesswork out of feeding your puppy well. Since growth-food formulas are designed to provide the nutrition that a growing puppy needs, it is unnecessary and, in fact, can prove harmful to add supplements to the diet. Research has shown that too much of certain vitamin supplements and minerals predispose a dog to skeletal problems. It's by no means a case of "if a little is good, a lot is better." At every stage of your dog's life, too much or too little in the way of nutrients can be harmful, which is why a manufactured complete food is the easiest way to know that your dog is getting what he needs.

Because of a young pup's small body and accordingly small digestive system, his daily portion will be divided up into small meals throughout the day. This can mean starting off with three or more meals a day and decreasing the number of meals as the pup matures. For the adult, dividing the day's food into two meals on a morning/evening schedule is healthier for the dog's digestion than one large daily portion and also reduces the risk of bloat, a potentially fatal condition that is discussed in detail in the healthcare chapter.

Dinnertime for hungry pups! The breeder starts the litter off on solid food as part of the weaning process.

You will get to know the daily portions that maintain your Komondor in good condition.

Regarding the feeding schedule, feeding the pup at the same times and in the same place each day is important for both housebreaking purposes and establishing the dog's everyday routine. As for the amount to feed, growing puppies generally need proportionately more food per body weight than their adult counterparts, but a pup should never be allowed to gain excess weight. Dogs of all ages should be kept in proper body condition, but extra weight can strain a pup's developing frame, causing skeletal problems.

Watch your pup's weight as he grows and, if the recommended amounts seem to be too much or too little for your pup, consult the vet about appropriate dietary changes. Keep in mind that treats, although small, can quickly add up throughout the day, contributing unnecessary calories. Treats are fine when used prudently; opt for dog treats specially formulated to be healthy or for nutritious snacks like small pieces of cheese or cooked chicken.

FEEDING THE ADULT DOG

For the adult (meaning physically mature) dog, feeding properly is about maintenance, not growth. Again, correct weight is a concern. Your dog should appear fit and should have an evident "waist." Weight gain or loss will be difficult to detect by sight under that coat, so you should evaluate his condition with regular hands-on examinations. His ribs should not be protruding (a sign of being underweight), but they should be covered by only a slight layer of fat. Under normal circumstances, an adult dog can be maintained fairly easily with a high-quality nutritionally complete adult-formula food.

Factor treats into your dog's overall daily caloric intake, and avoid offering table scraps. Not only are certain "people foods," like chocolate, nuts, grapes, raisins, onions and significant quantities of garlic, toxic to dogs but feeding from your plate also encourages begging and overeating. Overweight dogs are more prone to health problems; obesity can even take years off a dog's life. Resist the urge to overfeed and over-treat. Don't make unnecessary additions to your dog's diet, whether with tidbits or with extra vitamins and minerals.

The amount of food needed for proper maintenance will vary depending on the individual dog's activity level, but you will be able to tell whether the daily portions are keeping him in good shape. With the wide variety of good complete foods available, choosing what to feed is largely a matter of personal preference. Just as with the puppy, the adult dog should have consistency in his mealtimes and feeding place. In addition to a consistent routine, regular mealtimes also allow the owner to practice the important bloat preventives related to feeding and exercise. Regular mealtimes also allow the owner to see how much his dog is eating. If the dog seems never to be satisfied or, likewise, becomes uninterested in his food, the owner will know right away that something is wrong and can consult the vet.

DIETS FOR THE AGING DOG
A good rule of thumb is that once a dog has reached 75% of his expected lifespan, he has reached "senior citizen" or geriatric status. Your Komondor will be considered a senior at about 8 or 9 years of age; based on his size and breed-specific factors, he has a projected lifespan of about 12 years.

What does aging have to do with your dog's diet? No, he won't get a discount at the local diner's early-bird special. Yes, he will require some dietary changes to accommodate the changes that come along with increased age. One change is that the older dog's dietary needs become more similar to those of a puppy. Specifically, dogs can metabolize more protein as youngsters and seniors than in the adult-maintenance stage. Discuss with your vet whether you need to switch to a higher-protein or senior-formulated food or whether your current adult-dog food contains sufficient nutrition for the senior.

Watching the dog's weight remains essential, even more so in the senior stage. Older dogs are already more vulnerable to illness, and obesity only contributes to their susceptibility to problems. As the older dog becomes less active and, thus exercises less, his regular portions may cause him to gain weight. At this point, you may consider decreasing his daily food intake or switching to a reduced-calorie food. As with other changes, you should consult your vet for advice.

HOLD THE ONIONS
Sliced, chopped, grated; dehydrated, boiled, fried or raw; pearl, Spanish, white or red: onions can be deadly to your dog. The toxic effects of onions in dogs are cumulative for up to 30 days. A serious form of anemia, called Heinz body anemia, affects the red blood cells of dogs that have eaten onions. For safety (and better breath), dogs should avoid chives and scallions as well.

SPECIAL FEEDING CONSIDERATIONS FOR THE KOMONDOR

There are certain issues that seem to come up again and again with Komondor owners that we will discuss here. For one thing, Komondor puppies eat a lot. We tell people that dogs on the average gain ten pounds for each month of their life. A 4-week old puppy does not always weigh as much as 10 pounds, but by 8 weeks old, a good-sized puppy should weigh about 20 pounds, and at 3 months the puppy should weigh about 30 pounds, etc. However, by 9 months old and 90 pounds, he should be slowing down in weight gain.

Sometimes owners find that, at around four months old, their puppy is not eating well. Characteristically the pup seems very hungry, rushes to his food and takes a few bites, then backs off and does not finish his food. At this age, I suggest looking at his gums: if they are red and swollen, the problem is that he is teething and it hurts to bite down. The problem disappears when the teeth are in.

The next issue arises around nine months old. The dog is usually not finishing his kibble, and only a stupid Komondor would leave any food he gets, right? At this point the owner must evaluate how much he offers the puppy and how many daily meals are fed. We feed baby puppies four times a day. At eight weeks, they get three meals a day. When they start leaving food in their bowls or it is just more convenient for us, we change to two meals a day. We always prefer to feed our grown dogs twice a day, even though most would prefer a meal once a day. They seem to want their bigger meal in the evening. A very large Komondor (my Hunor was 31 inches and properly slim but not thin at 130 pounds) ate only 1.5 cups of kibble and a hamburger-sized amount of meat at each of his two meals. My 100-pound bitches get slightly less than 1 cup of kibble plus slightly less meat twice a day. Some owners tell me they offer three or more cups of

> **QUENCHING HIS THIRST**
> Is your dog drinking more than normal and trying to lap up everything in sight? Excessive drinking has many different causes. Obvious causes for a dog's being thirstier than usual are hot weather and vigorous exercise. However, if your dog is drinking more for no apparent reason, you could have cause for concern. Serious conditions like kidney or liver disease, diabetes and various types of hormonal problems can all be indicated by excessive drinking. If you notice your dog's being excessively thirsty, contact your vet at once. Hopefully there will be a simpler explanation, but the earlier a serious problem is detected, the sooner it can be treated, with a better rate of cure.

kibble at each of two meals; I doubt that most grown Komondors will want this much.

I grant you that my dogs, especially the older ones, are not as active as younger dogs or working dogs are, but Karika was always an active bitch while her sister Kincs never exerted herself and slept for most of the day, and they ate the same amount of food! If you feed a Komondor more than he needs, different dogs react differently: one dog will eat it all and have diarrhea, one will leave a good portion of whatever he likes least and, if his owner pampers him, one will end up getting "fussy" about food. If you "humor" the fussy eater, you will end up trying new things all the time. A better way is to cut down on the amount of food until your dog is hungry enough to clean his bowl at every meal. I seriously doubt that he will waste away before you solve his eating problem. The instructions given on most standard brands of kibble give amounts that no Komondor could possibly consume. Remember that most of the larger working breeds were bred by frugal peasants, and adult dogs are maintained on modest amounts of food. Also, livestock guard dogs do not overexert themselves, even when they are seriously guarding flocks.

DON'T FORGET THE WATER!
Regardless of what type of food he eats, there's no doubt that your Komondor needs plenty of water. Fresh cold water, in a clean bowl, should be available to your dog. There are special circumstances, such as during puppy house-breaking, when you will want to monitor your pup's water intake so that you will be able to predict when he will need to relieve himself, but water must be available to him nonetheless. Water is essential for hydration and proper body function just as it is in humans.

You will get to know how much your dog typically drinks in a day. Of course, in the heat or if exercising vigorously, he will be more thirsty and will drink more. However, if he begins to drink noticeably more water for no apparent reason, this could signal any of various problems, and you are advised to consult your vet.

A word of caution concerning

Fresh water is as important to your Kom's health as nutritious food.

your deep-chested dog's water intake: he should never be allowed to gulp water, especially at mealtimes. In fact, his water intake should be restricted to a few licks at mealtimes as a rule. This simple daily precaution can go a long way in protecting your dog from the dangerous and potentially fatal gastric torsion (bloat).

EXERCISE

We all know the importance of exercise for humans, so it should come as no surprise that it is essential for our canine friends as well. Now, regardless of your own level of fitness, get ready to assume the role of personal trainer for your dog. It's not as hard as it sounds, and it will have health benefits for you, too.

Just as with anything else you do with your dog, you must set a routine for his exercise. It's the same as your daily morning run before work or never missing the 7 P.M. aerobics class. If you plan it and get into the habit of actually doing it, it will become just another part of your day. Think of it as making daily exercise appointments with your dog, and stick to your schedule.

As a rule, dogs in normal health should have at least a half-hour of activity each day. Dogs with health or orthopedic problems may have specific limitations, so their exercise plans are best devised with the help of a vet. For healthy dogs, there are many ways to fit 30 minutes of activity into your day. Depending on your schedule, you may plan a 15-minute walk or activity session in the morning and again in the evening, or do it all at once in a half-hour session each day. Walking is the most popular way to exercise a dog (it's good for you, too!); other suggestions include retrieving games, jogging and disc-catching or other active games with his toys. Swimming is not a good way to exercise the Komondor,

> **EXERCISE WITH FRIENDS**
> Puppies grow best when they have plenty of space to exercise freely. Youngsters are active and benefit from playmates. When they get older, they need less exercise, but companion dogs will still enjoy a strenuous romp with a playmate or an owner with a toy even when they are old dogs. A working dog should be raised with his flock, and he must be carefully overseen so he does not harm fragile goats or even sheep, calves or colts.

Proper Care

because his coat becomes very heavy with water and takes a very long time to dry.

On that note, some precautions should be taken with a puppy's exercise. During his first year, when he is growing and developing, your Komondor should not be subject to activity that stresses his body. Short walks at a comfortable pace and play sessions in the yard are good for a growing pup, and his exercise can be increased as he grows up.

For overweight dogs, dietary changes and activity will help the goal of weight loss. (Sound familiar?) While they should of course be encouraged to be active, remember not to overdo it, as the excess weight is already putting strain on his vital organs and bones. As for highly active dogs, some of them never seem to tire! They will enjoy time spent with their owners doing things together.

When planning your dog's feeding and exercise schedule, it is essential to provide adequate periods of rest before and after eating to avoid stomach upset or the more serious gastric torsion (bloat), which can be fatal. For very active dogs, treats can be fed during rest periods to keep up the dog's energy in between meals, and plenty of water should be given. The dog needs time to settle down before and after any eating or drinking, so breaks should be factored in to the training program, exercise routine or work routine.

Your Kom will jump for joy over spending quality one-on-one time with you exercising outdoors.

Regardless of your dog's condition and activity level, exercise offers benefits to all dogs and owners. Consider the fact that dogs who are kept active are more stimulated both physically and mentally, meaning that they are less likely to become bored and lapse into destructive behavior. Also consider the benefits of one-on-one time with your dog every day, continually strengthening the bond between the two of you. Furthermore, exercising together will improve health and longevity for both of you. You both need exercise, and now you and your dog have a workout partner and motivator!

GROOMING

THE KOMONDOR'S CORDS
How does the coat get that way? We always say it grows that way, but this is only partly true. Komondors have a double coat. Cords are the

result of the coarser outer coat twisting initially around clumps of the finer puppy coat and later around the undercoat, which is similar to the puppy coat. Coats vary a great deal, depending on the ratio of undercoat to outer coat, but these days it is hard to find a Komondor that you cannot cord. Some coats seem to just simply grow into cords on their own, and you do not have a choice about how thick you want the cords to be. However, more Komondors need a lot of help from their owners at certain ages.

Shortly after birth, the puppy coat looks like old-fashioned marcelled waves; by a month old it looks mostly straight. Somewhere around eight or nine months old, you should find some coarser hair growing in and at the same time you will find that the hair is matting, especially in some areas: the ears, behind the ears and any area where limbs rub against the coat, such as under the arms and the legs. The chest is the last area to mat and then cord. I have seen the coarser outer coat grow in patches. Don't worry, this too will pass. A dog of mine that looked the worst at eight months old ended up with the best coat I ever had.

At this point, we do not recommend much bathing. If you bathe the dog at the wrong time, you can get really difficult mats. Instead, we separate the mats into divisions no smaller in diameter than your thumb. Remember that these divisions will tighten up when the coat gets wet, and you don't want the cords to get too thin at the base, as later the base has to be strong enough to hold heavier cords. Also, you can always separate cords that are too thick, but it is not easy to make them bigger. Usually, if you look carefully, you will see that the coat separates into layers, or you can separate it into layers easily. You can then just tear the layers into individual smaller areas. It is best if you make the cords by tearing, but in some areas the mats don't tear easily. At this point you need one or more tools: mat splitters, seam rippers and/or scissors. This involves cutting the coat into strips.

Start at the skin and cut outward. Often, if you cut an inch or so with scissors, you can tear the

Cords should be separated to the skin so you can easily check for fleas and ticks.

rest. Keep at it, but we suggest not trying to do the whole dog at once. Pick an area and stop before you or the dog gets tired. There is always another day. Then one day you will find that you have done the whole dog! At this point the dog looks a bit like a big pillow. Don't worry, these divisions will soon turn into cords. Everyone finds that although they have separated the whole coat nicely, a few days later it seems to have grown back together. Just keep at it, and one fine day, the cords will stay. Once the dog is really corded, usually by two years of age, it is not difficult to keep the coat in good shape. We try not to bathe the dogs more often than every other month. If we check the cords before and during the bath, that is all we have to do. The dogs love the attention you give them when they are being worked on. If you watch TV, they will sit at (or on) your feet and let you work away. Some dogs have definite preferences among TV programs. They really seem to like animal programs.

So now the dog is basically corded. What general maintenance is involved? At a minimum, you will need a crate, a dryer and grooming tools and supplies if you are to groom the dog yourself. You may have to groom the dog yourself, as few groomers know what to do with a Komondor. If you figure out a reasonable procedure, you may be able to show a groomer how to work on your dog. If you do not plan to show your dog, we suggest that you let the coat cord, help it cord and trim it back to about 3 inches in length all over the body once a year. This coat length (which a show dog will have at about three years of age) looks dignified and is easy to keep. If you opt to cut the dog all the way down, you will face mats as the coat grows back in. Three-inch cords will give you a coat that is easy to maintain. For this procedure, we suggest using cheap utility scissors, because cutting a whole coat, cord by cord, will destroy a good pair of scissors. Get a cheap pair and plan to throw it away after it does the job.

Some owners of working dogs shear the coat when they shear the sheep. However, other owners of working dogs, especially those in cold climates, keep cords on the dogs and just cut them back at intervals. Once the dog is corded, it is easy to check for ticks and other

Despite the full set of cords that seemingly cover the dog's eyes, the Kom can always see his groomer clearly.

parasites; this is not so easy if the coat grows out in mats.

Grooming Tools

I have been grooming Komondors since we got our first dog in 1967. For the last decade, I have had Cindy Adametz, a very gifted professional groomer, working on my dogs, usually with me helping. Cindy was trained at the Nash Academy, and she taught there as well. Our first Komondor was a real show dog, and we showed him a lot, so we washed him a lot. Marion and I did most of the washing, and sometimes our handler Bob Stebbins helped. We put in a raised, free-standing tub so that two people can work on the dog at the same time. The only thing lacking is a ramp, but this has not been a problem for us, because most of our dogs learn to jump into the tub. It has been a handicap for older dogs, but some have learned that if they put their front feet on the rim, we can easily boost them in. We have a mixometer and two outflows: one has a kitchen hand spray; the other has a regular hose, and we use a yard sprayer on it that can be changed into different patterns. We also have one hose end with a very gentle spray, good for faces on older dogs. We have built up an array of tools and products that we find useful. It might also be useful to let you in on our "secrets," which we do not mean to keep secret.

Tools for Grooming Youngsters: At the moment I have a young dog who was almost, but not totally, corded at 12 months. He is quite a lot of work. I know what works best on him, so I am writing this before I forget! You can use a mat splitter if you work well with it. I find I am a little afraid of it, so I use the largest seam ripper I can find and it works very well. I use a smaller seam ripper on the edges of the ears. I have not cut either the dog or myself with these, and they are very sharp. The other tool is a pair of scissors. In my experience, and just to reiterate, you do not want expensive professional scissors, which a corded coat will ruin; you want cheap but new and sharp ones, and Cindy and I prefer rather short blades.

We give puppies and youngsters very few baths. They tend to get dirty, and then when they dry, the

---

DO NOT COMB!

The hair of the Komondor is never combed. Combing would discourage the formation of cords. Large mats should be separated by tearing them apart. If the mats do not tear easily, tools like a mat splitter, a pair of scissors or a seam ripper are useful. The mats should be separated to the skin. Initially the mats should be no thinner than the diameter of your thumb. They tighten with age and with each washing and should not be too thin. They can always be divided into smaller cords later, if necessary, but they cannot be made thicker later.

Proper Care

An up-close look at proper adult Komondor cords. Note the thickness, as it is recommended that they be no thinner than the diameter of your thumb.

dirt falls off. Unless they roll in something repugnant, they do not have a doggy odor. Mud on the face or legs usually can be hosed off just with water. We keep our Komondors cleanable rather than clean. Little puppies do get washed a few times to get them used to the tub and to the dryer, but as soon as their hair starts to mat, we do not wash them until we have separated the cords. This is easiest with two people, of course.

You must get little ones used to having hair plucked from their ears, having their eyes cleaned and having their nails cut. A useful tool for pulling hair out of the ears is a Hairmostat®, which is a hemostat with no locking mechanism. It is helpful to put powder in the ears before you start pulling, as it gives you a better grip on the hairs. The dog's nails are cut while he is standing, usually in the bathtub after having been washed and rinsed, because after soaking in water the nails are softer and easier to cut. We prefer a plier-style nail clipper. Some owners are good with a grinder, but you have to be careful about catching hair in it. Good groomers almost never cut nails so short that they bleed, but perhaps in your grooming bag you have room for some nail-clotting solution; failing that, powder will do the trick. We keep medicated baby powder on hand; it is useful for many things.

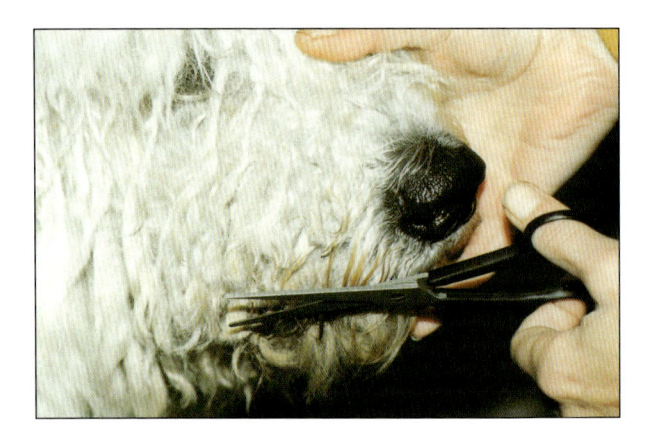

Scissors can be used to keep the facial furnishings looking tidy.

Clippers are used to shave the inside of the ear flaps, the belly, around the vulva or penis and around the anus. If you can use clippers to trim hair from between the foot pads, this is also good. Blunt scissors are also useful for trimming hair between the pads and various other places. In addition, we use good tweezers to get debris out of the coat.

You also need a crate for drying the dog. Ours have bottoms designed for this; they let air rise under the crate and therefore, under the wet dog. We also use a force dryer when the dog is standing in the tub. You need blotters for getting a lot of water out of the coat, and some towels initially in the crate. You also need standing dryers—we find we need two of them. That's a lot of equipment, but we do use all of these things.

BATHING

We have good water pressure; hopefully you do as well. Our procedure is to get hair out of the ears and clean them before we start a bath. We also take hair out of the pads, trim hair on the ear flaps and trim the coat if needed. We put cotton in the dog's ears after we clean them with witch hazel, and we put a drop of mineral oil in the dog's eyes to protect them from the suds. He then goes into the tub. We find we can rinse a lot of loose dirt off the dog with a strong spray head on the hose. If this is not feasible, we soak the dog in water into which we have put borax and some Oxydol crystal white detergent. If you can get the dog to lie down in this in the tub, it helps.

After soaking, we put clean water in the tub and, with the dog standing, we soap him up with dog shampoo. As we clean him, we can easily take any cords apart. If you do this when the dog is wet, the cords will stay separated better as they

The hair between the footpads should be trimmed. If the hair grows too long, it will cause the dog discomfort as well as collect debris that can lead to matting.

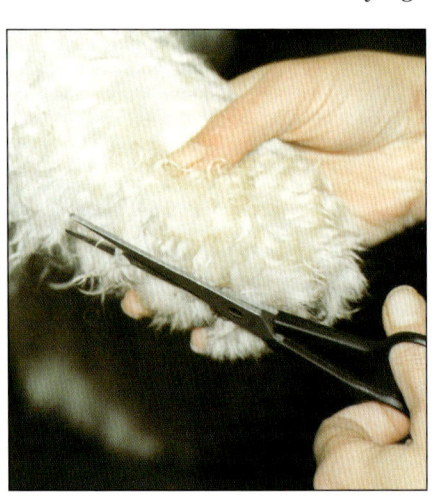

dry. We have used shampoos for white coats, but we have also used other products. Any Komondor can be allergic to any shampoo, so choose a shampoo and see how your dog does with it. After thorough soaping and work on the cords, we then rinse thoroughly—this is very important. Leaving soap in is very likely to cause allergic reactions. If the coat still feels like it is soapy, use a vinegar rinse. Just be sure to wash off the rinse.

Next comes blotting the cords. Synthetic towels do best; they get out more water and are easier on your hands than cotton towels. The longer you use blotters, the quicker the dog will dry. Also while the dog is being blotted, we can check any problems areas and treat them, if necessary. We finally use a force dryer while the dog is still in the tub; this again helps locate any skin problems. Before the dog leaves the tub, we let out the water and cut the dog's nails, which are now soft and cut easily. If the dog has dewclaws, be sure you check and cut them.

Next, we get the dog out of the tub and under the standing dryers. We put the dog in the crate with a layer of towels. We take out those towels in about an hour as they will be sopping wet. After this, we use an extra-large, extra-absorbent chamois (made for grooming) to catch any remaining dripping water. It takes hours to dry a mature corded coat, so part of the way through the process we take the dog out to relieve himself, then return him to the crate; at this point, the chamois is removed. When the dog is dry and he comes out of the crate, we apply powder to shaved areas like the ears and stomach to help avoid itchy skin.

The next day, I go over the cords and separate to the skin as needed. If you need to do any final clipping on the feet or face, you can do it at this point. After this whole process, our dogs seem to know that

The formation of cords is best accomplished during bathing, when the coat is wet.

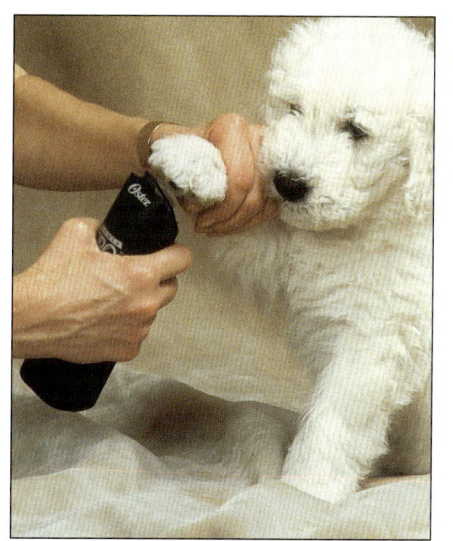

You can carefully neaten the Komondor's feet with an electric (or battery-operated) clipper.

The early stages of cord formation can be seen on this Komondor chow hound.

they are looking and smelling good, and they ask for a lot of touching and hugging.

EAR CLEANING
Any dog is grouchy if he has a sore ear or ears. Check your Komondor's ears routinely. In case of trouble, the following method has served us well over the years. Along with routine ear care, we also recommend an ear-wash formula by Dr. J.C. Blumenthal, popular with owners of many breeds. We have heard of at least one Komondor who seemed to be allergic to this ear wash, so proceed with caution the first time you use it.

If your Komondor scratches his ears or shakes his head a lot, be sure to look in his ears to see if they are inflamed or tender or if they have a brown discharge. A badly affected ear will also have an unpleasant odor. If the ear is full of hair, pull out as much as you can. You can use your fingers, tweezers, forceps or even pliers. After you have pulled the excess hair out, and/or when the ear is tender, use Panalog in the ear twice a day for a couple of days until the ear is no longer irritated. Then use the following ear wash to clean out the ear twice daily until it is clean and sweet-smelling. To use the ear wash, which is easiest to handle in a bottle with a small pouring spout, shake it well and pour about a teaspoon or two into one ear at a time. With your hand cupped behind the ear,

GROOMING PRODUCTS
Here is a list of useful products. I have marked indispensable items with *
- Hydrogen peroxide 3 % *
- Witch hazel*
- Rubbing alcohol*
- Mineral oil* (in a small bottle with a covered tip)
- Cotton: rolls and balls*
- Cotton swabs*
- Baby powder, medicated preferred*
- Borax
- White vinegar
- Ear cleaner* (we often use witch hazel for this)
- Eye cleaner
- Some type of skin disinfectant
- Bath oil*
- Shampoo*
- Stain removers*

massage it gently for a minute; you will hear the liquid squish around in the ear canal. Do both ears this way before you let the dog shake his head (best to do this outside!). Results are seen in just a few days. The ear wash ingredients are:
- Boric acid powder
- Isopropyl alcohol (rubbing alcohol)
- Gentian violet

In a 4-ounce bottle, put 1 1/4 teaspoons of boric acid powder and a few drops of gentian violet. Fill the bottle with isopropyl alcohol. All of the ingredients can be found at your local grocery store or drugstore. If you make it in quantity, use brown bottles (available from your pharmacist); for application, I prefer the bottles with the narrow tips, also available from the pharmacist. If you spill the ear wash on the dog's coat it will be lavender, but it wears off quickly.

By the way, if you get an urge to wipe the inside of your dog's ears or any other delicate area, do not use baby wipes or other wipes made for humans. In our experience, these can cause a lot of irritation. It is better to use old-fashioned witch hazel, which is not likely to cause any trouble.

We shave the undersides of our dogs' ears or have the groomer do it with clippers, but we don't do this with ears that are even a little tender. Very sore or infected ears may require having your vet clean them out. Once you get them clean, be sure to stay proactive with your dog's ear care. Keep up with routine checks and cleaning to prevent future problems.

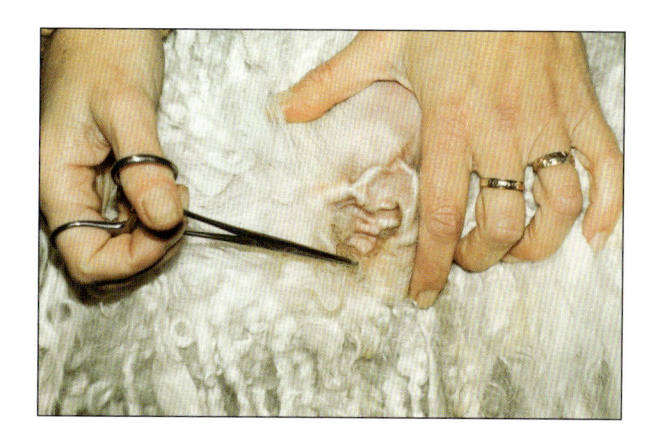

Remove excess hair from your Kom's ears. Be careful not to enter into the dog's ear canal.

EYE CARE

During grooming sessions, pay extra attention to the condition of your dog's eyes. If the area around the eyes is soiled or if tear staining has occurred, there are various cleaning agents made especially for this purpose. Look at the dog's eyes to make sure no debris has entered; dogs with large eyes and those who spend time outdoors are especially prone to this.

The signs of an eye infection are obvious: mucus, redness, puffiness, scabs or other signs of irritation. If your dog's eyes become infected, the vet will likely prescribe an antibiotic ointment for treatment. If you notice signs of more serious problems, such as opacities in the eye, which usually indicate cataracts, consult the vet at once.

KOMONDOR

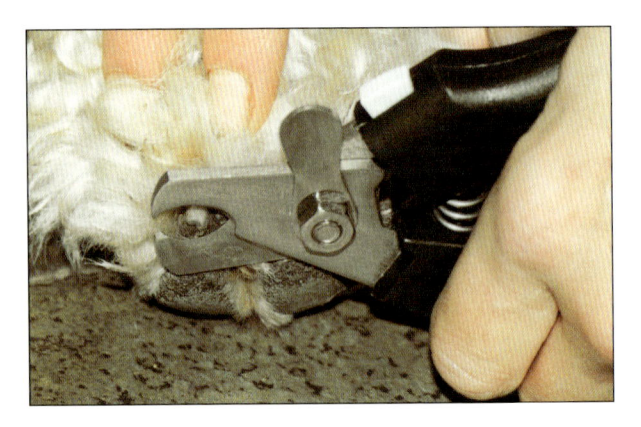

Special nail clippers designed for use on dogs are available at pet-supply shops. Many Kom owners find this "pliers" type easiest to use.

Taking time to pay attention to your dog's eyes will alert you in the early stages of any problem so that you can get your dog treatment as soon as possible. You could save your dog's sight!

A CLEAN SMILE

Another essential part of grooming is brushing your dog's teeth and checking his overall oral condition. Studies show that around 80% of dogs experience dental problems by two years of age, and the percentage is higher in older dogs. Therefore it is highly likely that your dog will have trouble with his teeth and gums unless you are proactive with home dental care.

The most common dental problem in dogs is plaque build-up. If not treated, this causes gum disease, infection and resultant tooth loss. Bacteria from these infections spread throughout the body, affecting the vital organs. Do you need much more convincing to start brushing your dog's teeth? If so, take a good whiff of your dog's breath, and read on.

Fortunately, home dental care is rather easy and convenient for pet owners. Specially formulated canine toothpaste is easy to find. You should use one of these toothpastes, not a product for humans. Some doggie pastes are even available in flavors appealing to dogs. If your dog likes the flavor, he will tolerate the process better, making things much easier for you! Doggie toothbrushes come in different sizes and are designed to fit the contour of a canine mouth. Rubber fingertip brushes fit right on one of your fingers and have rubber nodes to clean the teeth and massage the gums. This may be easier to handle, as it is akin to rubbing your dog's teeth with your finger.

As with other grooming tasks, accustom your Komondor pup to his dental care early on. Start

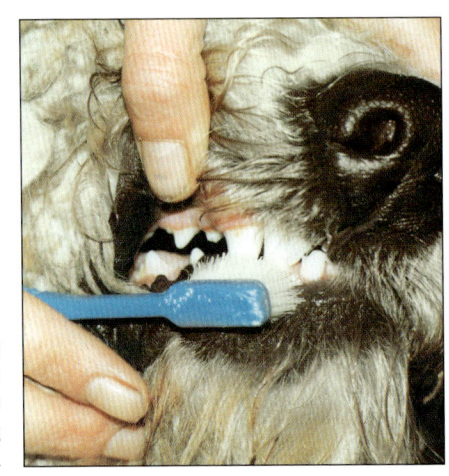

Make brushing your Komondor's teeth part of your regular grooming sessions.

Proper Care

gently, for a few minutes at a time, so that he gets used to the feel of the brush and to your handling his mouth. Offer praise and petting so that he looks at tooth-care time as a time when he gets extra love and attention. The routine should become second nature; he may not like it, but he should at least tolerate it.

Aside from brushing, offer dental toys to your dog and feed crunchy biscuits, which help to minimize plaque. Rope toys have the added benefit of acting like floss as the dog chews. At your adult dog's yearly check-ups, the vet will perform a complete check for any problems and possibly a thorough tooth scraping. Proper care of your dog's teeth will ensure that you will enjoy your dog's smile for many years to come. The next time your dog goes to give you a hello kiss, you'll be glad you spent the time caring for his teeth.

THE OTHER END

Dogs sometime have troubles with their anal glands, which are sacs located beside the anal vent. These should empty when a dog has normal bowel movements; if they don't, they can become full or impacted, causing discomfort. Owners often are alarmed to see their dogs scooting across the floor, dragging their behinds behind; this is just a dog's attempt to empty the glands himself.

Some brave owners attempt to evacuate their dogs' anal glands themselves during grooming, but no one will tell you that this is a pleasant task! Thus many owners prefer to make the trip to the vet to have the vet take care of the problem; owners whose dogs visit a groomer can have this done by the groomer if he offers this as part of his services. Regardless, don't neglect the dog's other end in your home-care routine. Look for scooting, licking or other signs of discomfort "back there" to ascertain whether the anal glands need to be emptied.

IDENTIFICATION

You love your Komondor and want to keep him safe. Of course you take every precaution to prevent his escaping from the yard or becoming lost or stolen. You have a sturdy high fence and you always

Tattooing is a permanent method of ID that works best when the tattoo is placed in a visible area on the dog.

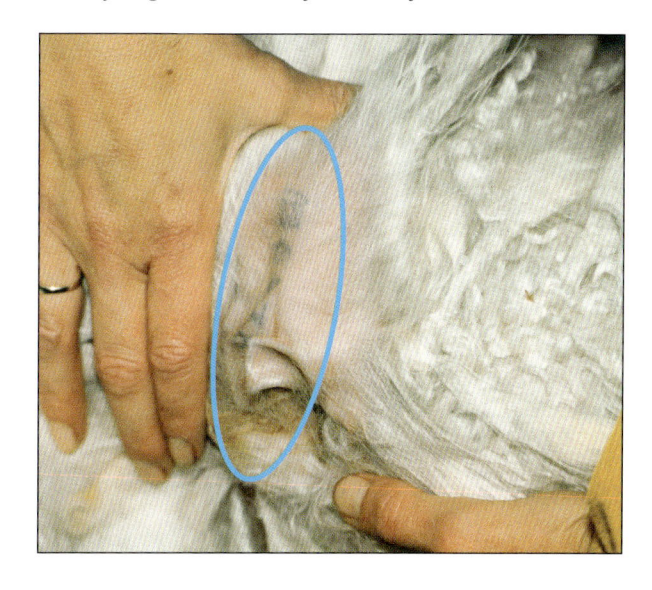

> **CAR CAUTION**
> You may like to bring your canine companion along on the daily errands, but if you will be running in and out from place to place and can't bring him indoors with you, leave him at home. Your dog should never be left alone in the car, not even for a minute—never! We've mentioned the Kom's protective nature in the car; plus, a car heats up very quickly, and even a cracked-open window will not help. In fact, leaving the window cracked will be dangerous if the dog becomes uncomfortable and tries to escape. When in doubt, leave your dog home, where you know he will be safe.

keep your dog on lead when out and about in public places. If your dog is not properly identified, however, you are overlooking a major aspect of his safety. We hope to never be in a situation where our dog is missing, but we should practice prevention in the unfortunate case that this happens; identification greatly increases the chances of your dog's being returned to you.

There are several ways to identify your dog. First, the traditional dog tag should be a staple in your dog's wardrobe, attached to his everyday collar. Tags can be made of sturdy plastic and various metals and should include your contact information so that a person who finds the dog can get in touch with you right away to arrange his return. Many people today enjoy the wide range of decorative tags available, so have fun and create a tag to match your dog's personality. Of course, it is important that the tag stays on the collar, so have a secure "O" ring attachment; you also can explore the type of tag that slides right onto the collar.

In addition to the ID tag, which every dog should wear even if identified by another method, two other forms of identification have become popular: microchipping and tattooing. In microchipping, a tiny scannable chip is painlessly inserted under the dog's skin. The number is registered to you so that, if your lost dog turns up at a clinic or shelter, the chip can be scanned to retrieve your contact information.

The advantage of the microchip is that it is a permanent form of ID, but there are some factors to consider. Several different companies make microchips, and not all are compatible with the others' scanning devices. It's best to find a company with a universal microchip that can be read by scanners made by other companies as well. It won't do any good to have the dog chipped if the information cannot be retrieved. Also, not every humane society, shelter and clinic is equipped with a scanner, although more and more facilities are equipping themselves. In fact, many shelters microchip dogs that they adopt out to new homes.

Because the microchip is not visible to the eye, the dog must wear a tag that states that he is microchipped so that whoever picks him up will know to have him scanned. The microchip ID tag typically also includes the dog's microchip number and the phone number of the registry.

Though less popular than microchipping, tattooing is another permanent method of ID for dogs, but this is not very effective for Koms. There is *no* conspicuous area to tattoo except the ear, and Komondors do not like strangers looking in their ears.

BOARDING
Today there are many options for dog owners who need someone to care for their dogs in certain circumstances. While many think of boarding their dogs as something to do when away on vacation, many others use the services of doggie "daycare" facilities, dropping their dogs off to spend the day while they are at work. Many of these facilities offer both long-term and daily care. Many go beyond just boarding and cater to all sorts of needs, with on-site grooming, veterinary care, training classes and even "web-cams" where owners can log onto the Internet and check out what their dogs are up to. Most dogs enjoy the activity and time spent with other dogs.

Your Komondor will want to go everywhere with you; it is up to you to make it as comfortable and safe as possible for him regardless of the means of travel.

Before you need to use such a service, check out the ones in your area. Make visits to see the facilities, meet the staff, discuss fees and available services and see whether this is a place where you think your dog will be happy. It is best to do your research in advance so that you're not stuck at the last minute, forced into making a rushed decision without knowing whether the kennel that you've chosen meets your standards. You also can check with your veterinarian's office to see whether they offer boarding for their clients or can recommend a good kennel in the area.

The kennel will need to see proof of your dog's health records and vaccinations so as not to spread illness from dog to dog. Your Komondor also will need proper identification. Owners usually experience some separation anxiety the first time they have to leave their dog in someone else's care, so it's reassuring to know that the kennel you choose is run by experienced, caring, true dog people.

Your vet can probably recommend a local kennel in which you can board your Kom. The kennel should be clean and professionally run, with adequate space and attention for each dog.

TRAINING YOUR

KOMONDOR

By Bardi McLennan

BASIC TRAINING PRINCIPLES: PUPPY VS. ADULT

There's a big difference between training an adult dog and training a young puppy. With a young puppy, everything is new! At eight to ten weeks of age, he will be experiencing many things, and he has nothing with which to compare these experiences. Up to this point, he has been with his dam and littermates, not one-on-one with people except in his interactions with his breeder and visitors to the litter.

When you first bring the puppy home, he is eager to please you. This means that he accepts doing things your way. During the next couple of months, he will absorb the basis of everything he needs to know for the rest of his life. This early age is even referred to as the "sponge" stage. After that, for the next 18 months, it's up to you to reinforce good manners by building on the foundation that you've established. Once your puppy is reliable in basic commands and behavior and has reached the appropriate age, you may gradually introduce him to some of the interesting sports, games and activities available to pet owners and their dogs.

Raising your puppy is a family affair. Each member of the family must know what rules to set forth for the puppy and how to use the same one-word commands to mean exactly the same thing every time. Even if yours is a large family, one person will soon be considered by the pup to be the leader, the alpha person in his

Training can take a lot out of a young Kom; be sure not to overdo it and also to provide some quiet time for your little student.

KOMONDOR

Training your dog can be a family affair, but it is of utmost importance that the training rules for the dog are consistently reinforced by all members of the family.

pack, the "boss" who must be obeyed. Often that highly regarded person turns out to be the one who feeds the puppy. Food ranks very high on the puppy's list of important things! That's why your puppy is rewarded with small treats along with verbal praise when he responds to you correctly. As the puppy learns to do what you want him to do, the food rewards are gradually eliminated and only the praise remains. If you were to keep up with the food treats, you could have two problems on your hands—an obese dog and a beggar.

Training begins the minute your Komondor puppy steps through the doorway of your home, so don't make the mistake of putting the puppy on the floor and telling him by your actions to "Go for it! Run wild!" Even if this is your first puppy, you must act as if you know what you're doing: be the boss. An uncertain pup may be terrified to move, while a bold one will be ready to take you at your word and start plotting to destroy the house! Before you collected your puppy, you decided where his own special place would be, and that's where to put him when you first arrive home. Give him a house tour after he has investigated his area and had a nap and a bathroom "pit stop."

It's worth mentioning here that, if you've adopted an adult dog that is completely trained to your liking, lucky you! You're off

THE RIGHT START

The best advice for a potential dog owner is to start with the very best puppy that money can buy. Don't shop around for a bargain in the newspaper. You're buying a companion, not a used car or a second-hand appliance. The purchase price of the dog represents a very significant part of the investment, but this is indeed a very small sum compared to the expenses of maintaining the dog in good health. If you purchase a well-bred, healthy and sound puppy, you will be starting right. An unhealthy puppy can cost you thousands of dollars in unnecessary veterinary expenses and, possibly, a fortune in heartbreak as well.

the hook! However, if that dog spent his life up to this point in a kennel, or even in a good home but without any real training, be prepared to tackle the job ahead. A dog three years of age or older with no previous training cannot be blamed for not knowing what he was never taught. While the dog is trying to understand and learn your rules, at the same time he has to unlearn many of his previously self-taught habits and general view of the world.

Working with a professional trainer will speed up your progress with an adopted adult dog. You'll need patience, too. Some new rules may be close to impossible for the dog to accept. After all, he's been successful so far by doing everything his way! (Patience again.) He may agree with your instruction for a few days and then slip back into his old ways, so you must be just as consistent and understanding in your teaching as you would be with a puppy. (More patience needed yet again!) Your dog has to learn to pay attention to your voice, your family, the daily routine, new smells, new sounds and, in some cases, even a new climate.

One of the most important things to find out before adopting an adult Komondor is his reaction to children (yours and others), strangers and your friends and how he acts upon meeting other dogs. If he was not socialized with dogs as a puppy, this could be a major problem. This does not mean that he's a "bad" dog, a vicious dog or an aggressive dog; rather, it means that he has no idea how to read another dog's body language. There's no way for him to tell whether the other dog is a friend or foe. Survival instinct takes over, telling him to attack first and ask questions later. This definitely calls for professional help and, even then, may not be a behavior that can be corrected 100% reliably (or even at all). If you have a puppy, this is why it is so very important to introduce him properly to other puppies and "dog-friendly" adult dogs.

You will have a much easier time training your adult Kom if he looks up to you as his trusted leader.

HOUSE-TRAINING YOUR KOMONDOR

Dogs are "touch-sensitive" when it comes to house-training. In other words, they respond to the surface on which they are given approval to eliminate. The choice is yours (the dog's version is in parentheses): The lawn (including the neighbors' lawns)? A bare patch of earth under a tree (where people like to sit and relax in the summertime)? Concrete steps or patio (all sidewalks, garages and basement floors)? The curbside (watch out for cars)? A small area of crushed stone in a corner of the yard (mine!)? The latter is the best choice if you can manage it, because it will remain strictly for the dog's use and is easy to keep clean.

Although some people start out with paper-training indoors and switch over to an outdoor surface as the puppy matures and gains control over his need to eliminate, this is not an advisable start for Komondors. Most Komondors do better if you skip the paper-training; they are such conservative dogs that once they get used to something, it can be very hard to train them to do something new.

When Your Puppy's "Got to Go"

Your puppy's need to relieve himself is seemingly non-stop, but signs of improvement will be seen each week. From 8 to 10 weeks old, the puppy will have to be taken outside every time he wakes up, about 10–15 minutes after every meal and after every period of play—all day long, from first thing in the morning until his bedtime! That's a total of ten or more trips per day to teach the puppy where it's okay to relieve himself. With that schedule in mind, you can see that house-training a young puppy is not a part-time job. It requires someone to be home all day.

If that seems overwhelming or impossible, do a little planning. For example, plan to pick up your puppy at the start of a vacation period. If you can't get home in the middle of the day, plan to hire a dog-sitter or ask a neighbor to come over to take the pup outside, feed him his lunch and then take him out again about ten or so minutes after he's eaten. Also make arrangements with that or another person to be your "emergency" contact if you have to stay late on the job. Remind yourself—repeatedly—that this hectic schedule improves as the puppy gets older.

Home within a Home

Your Komondor puppy needs to be confined to one secure, puppy-proof area when no one is able to watch his every move. Generally the kitchen is the place of choice because the floor is washable. Likewise, it's a busy family area that will accustom the pup to a variety of noises, everything from pots and pans to the telephone, blender and dishwasher. He will also be enchanted by the smell of your cooking (and will never be critical when you burn something). A crate within the room of choice is the best means of confinement for a young pup. He can see out and has a certain amount of space in which to move about, but he is safe from dangerous things like electrical cords, heating units, trash baskets or open kitchen-supply cabinets. Place the crate where the puppy will not get a blast of heat or air conditioning.

In the crate you can put a few toys. A water bowl can be hung at a convenient height on the side of the crate so it won't become a splashing pool for an innovative puppy. You may want to feed him in his crate as well.

Crates are something that pet owners are at last getting used to for their dogs. Wild or domestic canines have always preferred to sleep in den-like safe spots, and that is exactly what the crate provides. How often have you seen adult dogs that choose to sleep under a table or chair even though they have full run of the house? It's the den connection.

In your "happy" voice, use the word "Crate" every time you put the pup into his den. If he's new to a crate, toss in a small biscuit

> **DAILY SCHEDULE**
> How many relief trips does your puppy need per day? A puppy up to the age of 14 weeks will need to go outside about 8 to 12 times per day! You will have to take the pup out any time he starts sniffing around the floor or turning in small circles, as well as after naps, meals, games and lessons or whenever he's released from his crate. Once the puppy is 14 to 22 weeks of age, he will require only 6 to 8 relief trips. At the ages of 22 to 32 weeks, the puppy will require about 5 to 7 trips. Adult dogs typically require 4 relief trips per day, in the morning, afternoon, evening and late at night.

for him to chase the first few times. At night, after he's been outside, he should sleep in his crate. The crate may be kept in his designated area at night or, if you want to be sure to hear those wake-up yips in the morning, put the crate in a corner of your bedroom. However, don't make any response whatsoever to whining or crying. If he's completely ignored, he'll settle down and get to sleep.

Some owners find that good bedding for a young puppy is an old folded bath towel or an old blanket, something that is easily washable and disposable if necessary ("accidents" will happen!). Never put newspapers in the Kom puppy's crate; he will eat them. Also, those old ideas about adding a clock to replace his mother's heartbeat or a hot-water bottle to replace her warmth, are just that—old ideas. The clock could drive the puppy nuts, and the hot-water bottle could end up as a very soggy waterbed! An extremely good breeder would have introduced your puppy to the crate by letting two pups sleep together for a couple of nights, followed by several nights alone. How thankful you will be if you found that breeder!

Safe toys in the pup's crate or area will keep him occupied, but monitor their condition closely.

> **CREATURES OF HABIT**
>
> Canine behaviorists and trainers aptly describe dogs as "creatures of habit," meaning that dogs respond to structure in their daily lives and welcome a routine. Do not interpret this to mean that dogs enjoy endless repetition in their training sessions. Dogs get bored just as humans do. Keep training sessions interesting and exciting. Vary the commands and the locations in which you practice. Give short breaks for play in between lessons. A bored student will never be the best performer in the class.

Discard any toys that show signs of being chewed to bits. Squeaky parts, bits of stuffing or plastic or any other small pieces can cause intestinal blockage or possibly choking if swallowed.

PROGRESSING WITH POTTY-TRAINING
After you've taken your puppy out and he has relieved himself in the area you've selected, he can have some free time with the family as long as there is someone responsible for watching him. That doesn't mean just someone in the same room who is watching TV or busy on the computer but one person who is doing nothing other than keeping an eye on the pup, playing with him on the floor and helping him understand his position in the pack.

This first taste of freedom will

Use gates in your home to keep your Kom in areas that you deem safe and appropriate. Be sure to have sturdy gates for this large, powerful breed.

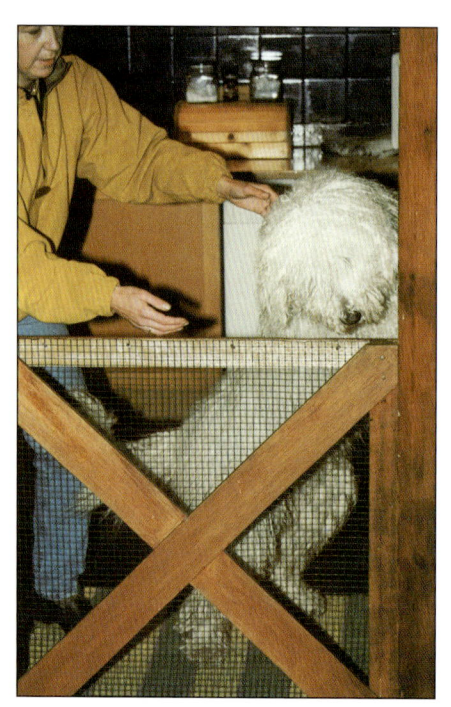

let you begin to set the house rules. If you don't want the dog on the furniture, now is the time to prevent his first attempts to jump up onto the couch. The word to use in this case is "Off," not "Down." "Down" is the word you will use to teach the down position, which is something entirely different.

Most corrections at this stage come in the form of simply distracting the puppy. Instead of telling him "No" for "Don't chew the carpet," distract the chomping puppy with a toy and he'll forget about the carpet.

As you are playing with the pup, do not forget to watch him closely and pay attention to his body language. Whenever you see him begin to circle or sniff, take the puppy outside to relieve himself. Praise him as he eliminates in the chosen area while he actually is in the act of relieving himself. Three seconds after he has finished is too late! You'll be praising him for running toward you, picking up a toy or whatever he may be doing at that moment, and that's not what you want to be praising him for. Timing is a vital tool in all dog training. Use it!

The next time you bring him outside, scent will attract him to his relief spot. That scent attraction is also why it's so important to clean up any messes made in the house by using a product specially made to eliminate the odor of dog urine and droppings. If the puppy smells the site of a previous potty accident indoors, he will be attracted to "go" there again. Regular household cleansers won't do the trick. Pet shops sell the best pet deodorizers. Invest in the largest container you can find.

As we've mentioned, scent attraction eventually will lead your pup to his chosen spot outdoors; this is the basis of outdoor training. Thus you do best if you take him to a spot where he has eliminated previously. When you take your puppy outside to relieve himself,

Very young puppies need to relieve themselves often and have very little control. Their control, of course, improves with age and training.

An attentive dog is the best student. Choose a distraction-free area for training, and make sure that your Kom's attention is focused on the lesson at hand.

use a one-word command such as "Outside" or "Go-potty" (that's one word to the puppy!) as you attach his leash. Then lead him to his area. Now comes the hard part—hard for you, that is. Just stand there until he urinates and defecates. Move him a few feet in one direction or another if he's just sitting there looking at you, but remember that this is neither playtime nor time for a walk. This is strictly a business trip! Then, as he circles and squats (remember your timing!), give him a quiet "Good dog" as praise. If you start to jump for joy, ecstatic over his performance, he'll do one of two things: either he will stop midstream, as it were, or he'll do it again for you—in the house—and expect you to be just as delighted!

Give him five minutes or so and, if he doesn't go in that time, take him back indoors to his confined area and try again in another ten minutes or immediately if you see him sniffing and circling. By careful observation, you'll soon work out a successful schedule.

Accidents, by the way, are just that—accidents. Clean them up quickly and thoroughly, without comment, after the puppy has been taken outside to finish his business and then put back into his area or crate. Putting him in the crate should never be a form of punishment, however; he is just getting some quiet time while you clean up. If you witness an accident in progress, say "No!" in a stern voice and get the pup outdoors immediately. No punishment is needed. You and your puppy are just learning each other's language, and sometimes it's easy to miss a puppy's message. Chalk it up to experience and watch more closely from now on.

KEEPING THE PACK ORDERLY
Discipline is a form of training that brings order to life. For example, military discipline is what allows the soldiers in an

Training

> **POTTY COMMAND**
>
> Most dogs love to please their masters; there are no bounds to what dogs will do to make their owners happy. The potty command is a good example of this theory. If toileting on command makes the master happy, then more power to him. Puppies will obligingly piddle if it really makes their keepers smile. Some owners can be creative about which word they will use to command their dogs to relieve themselves. Some popular choices are "Potty," "Tinkle," "Piddle," "Let's go," "Hurry up" and "Toilet." Give the command every time your puppy goes into position and the puppy will begin to associate his business with the command.

army to work as one. Discipline is a form of teaching and, in dogs, is the basis of how the successful pack operates. Each member knows his place in the pack and all respect the leader, or alpha dog. It is essential for your puppy that you establish this type of relationship, with you as the alpha, or leader. It is a form of social coexistence that all canines recognize and accept. Discipline, therefore, is never to be confused with punishment. When you teach your puppy how you want him to behave, and he behaves properly and you praise him for it, you are disciplining him with a form of positive reinforcement.

For a dog, rewards come in the form of praise, a smile, a cheerful tone of voice, a few friendly pats or a rub of the ears. Rewards are also small food treats. Obviously, that does not mean bits of regular dog food. Instead, treats are very small bits of special things like cheese or pieces of soft dog treats. The idea is to reward the dog with something very small that he can taste and swallow, providing instant positive reinforcement. If he has to take time to chew the treat, by the time he is finished he will have forgotten what he did to earn it!

Your puppy should never be physically punished. The displeasure shown on your face and in your voice is sufficient to signal to the pup that he has done

A dog the size of the Komondor must be trained. It would be impossible to walk an adult Komondor who didn't know how to behave on leash.

something wrong. He wants to please everyone higher up on the social ladder, especially his leader, so a scowl and harsh voice will take care of the error. Growling out the word "Shame!" when the pup is caught in the act of doing something wrong is better than the repetitive "No." Some dogs hear "No" so often that they begin to think it's their name! By the way, do not use the dog's name when you're correcting him. His name is reserved to get his attention for something pleasant about to take place.

There are punishments that have nothing to do with you. For example, your dog may think that chasing cats is one reason for his existence. You can try to stop it as much as you like but without success, because it's such fun for the dog. But one good hissing, spitting swipe of a cat's claws across the dog's nose will put an end to the game forever. Intervene only when your dog's eyeball is seriously at risk. Cat scratches can cause permanent damage to an innocent but annoying puppy.

PUPPY KINDERGARTEN

COLLAR AND LEASH

Before you begin your Komondor puppy's education, he must be used to his collar and leash. Choose a collar for your puppy that is secure but not heavy or bulky. He won't enjoy training if he's uncomfortable. A flat buckle collar is okay for everyday wear and for initial puppy training. We prefer light nylon choke collars. For older dogs, there are several types of training collars such as the martingale, which is a double loop that tightens slightly around the neck. We prefer a light chain choke collar but only after you have been specifically shown how to put it on and how to use it.

The author prefers a 6-foot leather lead, of either $1/2$-inch or $5/8$-inch width, although some

Before training can begin, your Kom must be comfortable with his collar and leash.

Training

trainers use a lightweight 6-foot woven cotton or nylon training leash that can fold up easily in your hand and is comfortable to hold. There are lessons in which the dog will start off 6 feet away from you at the end of the leash. The leash used to take the puppy outside to relieve himself can be shorter because you don't want him to roam away from his area. The shorter leash can also be the one to use when you walk the puppy.

If you've been wise enough to enroll in a puppy kindergarten training class, suggestions will be made as to the best collar and leash for your young puppy. I say "wise" because your puppy will be in a class with puppies in his age range (up to five months old) of all breeds and sizes. It's the perfect way for him to learn the right way (and the wrong way) to interact with other dogs as well as their people. You cannot teach your puppy how to interpret another dog's sign language. For a first-time puppy owner, these socialization classes are invaluable. For experienced dog owners, they are a real boon to further training.

Attention

You've been using the dog's name since the minute you collected him from the breeder, so you should be able to get his attention by saying his name—with a big

LEASH TRAINING

House-training and leash training go hand in hand, literally. When taking your puppy outside to do his business, lead him there on his leash. Unless an emergency potty run is called for, do not whisk the puppy up into your arms and take him outside. If you have a fenced yard, you have the advantage of letting the puppy loose to go out, but it's better to put the dog on the leash and take him to his designated place in the yard until he is reliably house-trained. Taking the puppy for a walk is the best way to house-train a dog. The dog will associate the walk with his time to relieve himself, and the exercise of walking stimulates the dog's bowels and bladder. Dogs that are not trained to relieve themselves on a walk may hold it until they get back home, which of course defeats half the purpose of the walk.

smile and in an excited tone of voice. His response will be the puppy equivalent of "Here I am! What are we going to do?" Your immediate response (if you haven't guessed by now) is "Good dog." Rewarding him at the moment he pays attention to you teaches him the proper way to respond when he hears his name.

A SIMPLE "SIT"
When you command your dog to sit, use the word "Sit." Do not say "Sit down," as your dog will not know whether you mean "Sit" or "Down," or maybe you mean both. Be clear in your instructions to your dog; use one-word commands and always be consistent.

EXERCISES FOR A BASIC CANINE EDUCATION

THE SIT EXERCISE
There are several ways to teach the puppy to sit. The first one is to catch him whenever he is about to sit and, as his backside nears the floor, say "Sit, good dog!" That's positive reinforcement and, if your timing is sharp, he will learn that what he's doing at that second is connected to your saying "Sit" and that you think he's clever for doing it!

Another method is to start with the puppy on his leash. Some dogs require gentle pressure on their hindquarters with the left hand, in which case the dog should be on your left side. When he sits, say "Sit, good dog" and then give him the treat and lots of praise. After a few times, you should be able to show the dog a treat in the open palm of your hand, raise your hand waist-high as you say "Sit" and have him sit. Here you have taught him two things at the same time. Both the verbal command and the motion of the hand are signals for the sit. Your puppy is watching you almost more than he is listening to you, so what you do is just as important as what you say.

Don't save any of these drills only for training sessions. Use them as much as possible at odd times during a normal day. The dog should always sit before being given his food dish. He should sit to let you go through a doorway first, when the doorbell rings or when you stop to speak to someone on the street.

THE DOWN EXERCISE
Before beginning to teach the down command, you must consider how the dog feels about this exercise. To him, "down" is a submissive position. Being flat on the floor with you standing over him is not his idea of fun. It's up

Training

to you to let him know that, while it may not be fun, the reward of your approval is worth his effort.

Here is one method: Start with the puppy on your left side in a sit position. Hold the leash right above his collar in your left hand. Have an extra-special treat, such as a small piece of cooked chicken or hot dog, in your right hand. Place it at the end of the pup's nose and steadily move your hand down and forward along the ground. Hold the leash to prevent a sudden lunge for the food. As the puppy goes into the down position, say "Down" very gently. Have the pup maintain the down position for several seconds. If he tries to get up immediately, place your hands on his shoulders and press down gently, giving him a very quiet "Good dog." As you progress with this lesson, increase the "down time" until he will hold it until you say "Okay" (his cue for release). Practice this one in the house at various times throughout the day.

There are other methods for teaching the down. A strong man may just push the puppy down, and the Kom may not object. I have seen a trainer have a dog sit and stay on a fairly long lead. With the lead in his right hand, he put his left foot on the lead so it could run beneath his instep. Then, in a firm voice, he gave the command "Down." At the same time, he pulled up with his right hand and pushed down with his left hand across the dog's shoulders. The dog seemed surprised to find he was lying down, but he was not frightened. The trainer then urged the dog to remain in the down position for a few minutes, praising him gently and stroking his head. Only after the dog seemed relaxed did the

Produce a tasty treat and watch your Kom's attention span grow.

trainer let him get up. The trick is to get the dog to stay down and then reward him for staying in position.

By increasing the length of time during which the dog must maintain the down position, you'll find many uses for it. For example, he can lie at your feet in the vet's office or anywhere that both of you have to wait, when you are on the phone, while the family is eating and so forth. If you progress to training for competitive obedience, he'll already be all set for the exercise called the "long down."

THE STAY EXERCISE

You can teach your Komondor to stay in the sit, down and stand positions. To teach the sit/stay, have the dog sit on your left side. Hold the leash at waist level in your left hand and let the dog know that you have a treat in your closed right hand. Step forward on your right foot as you say "Stay." Immediately turn and stand directly in front of the dog, keeping your right hand up high so he'll keep his eye on the treat hand and maintain the sit position for a count of five. Return to your original position and offer the reward.

Increase the length of the sit/stay each time until the dog can hold it for at least 30 seconds without moving. After about a week of success, move out on your right foot and take two steps before turning to face the dog. Give the "Stay" hand signal (left palm up, facing the dog's head) as you leave. He gets the treat when you return and he holds the sit/stay. Increase the distance that you walk away from him before turning until you reach

DOWN

"Down" is a harsh-sounding word and a submissive posture in dog body language, thus presenting two obstacles in teaching the down command. When the dog is about to flop down on his own, tell him "Good down." Pups that are not good about being handled learn better by having food lowered in front of them. A dog that trusts you can be gently guided into position. When you give the command "Down," be sure to say it sweetly!

the length of your training leash. But don't rush it! Go back to the beginning if he moves before he should. No matter what the lesson, never be upset by having to back up for a few days. The repetition and practice are what will make your dog reliable in these commands. It won't do any good to move on to something more difficult if the command is not mastered at the easier levels. Above all, even if you do get frustrated, never let your puppy know! Always keep a positive, upbeat attitude during training, which will transmit to your dog for positive results.

The down/stay is taught in the same way once the dog is completely reliable and steady with the down command. Again, don't rush it. With the dog in the down position on your left side, step out on your right foot as you say "Stay." Return by walking around in back of the dog and into your original position. While you are training, it's okay to murmur something like "Hold on" to encourage him to stay put. When the dog will stay without moving when you are at a distance of 3 or 4 feet, begin to increase the length of time before you return. Be sure he holds the down on your return until you say "Okay." At that point, he gets his treat—just so he'll remember for next time that it's not over until it's over.

THE COME EXERCISE

No command is more important to the safety of your Komondor than "Come." It is what you should say every single time you see the puppy running toward you: "Bodi, come! Good dog." During playtime, run a few feet away from the puppy and turn and tell him to "Come" as he is already running to you. You can go so far as to teach your puppy two things at once if you squat down and hold out your arms. As the pup gets close to you and you're saying "Good dog," bring your right arm in about waist high. Now he's also learning the hand signal, an excellent device should you be on the phone when you need to get him to come to you. You'll also both be one step ahead when you enter obedience classes.

"Stay" is a necessary command for your dog's behavior and safety.

When the puppy responds to your well-timed "Come," try it with the puppy on the training leash. This time, catch him off-guard, while he's sniffing a leaf or watching a bird: "Bodi, come!" You may have to pause for a split second after his name to be sure you have his attention. If the puppy shows any sign of confusion, give the leash a mild jerk and take a couple of steps backward. Do not repeat the command. In this case, you should say "Good come" as he reaches you.

That's the number-one rule of training. Each command word is given just once. Anything more is nagging. You'll also notice that all commands are one word only. Even when they are actually two words, you say them as one.

Never call the dog to come to you—with or without his name—if you are angry or intend to correct him for some misbehavior. When correcting the pup, you go to him. Your dog must always connect "Come" with something pleasant and with your approval; then you can rely on his response.

Puppies, like children, have notoriously short attention spans, so don't overdo it with any of the training. Keep each lesson short. Break it up with a quick run around the yard or a ball toss, repeat the lesson and quit as soon as the pup gets it right. That way, you will always end with a "Good dog."

Life isn't perfect and neither are puppies. A time will come, often around ten months of age, when he'll become "selectively deaf" or choose to "forget" his name. He may respond by wagging his tail (and even seeming to smile at you) with a look that says "Make me!" Laugh, throw his favorite toy and skip the lesson you had planned. Pups will be pups!

THE HEEL EXERCISE

The second most important command to teach, after the come, is the heel. When you are walking your growing puppy, you need to be in control. If you don't train your Komondor while he is still small and easy to handle, you will end up with a full-grown dog who is more than capable of pulling

Reinforcing verbal commands with hand signals is a very effective way of getting your dog to follow. This Kom is being called to come from a sit/stay.

you down the street. Your eight- to ten-week-old puppy will probably follow you everywhere, but that's his natural instinct, not your control over the situation. However, any time he does follow you, you can say "Heel" and be ahead of the game, as he will learn to associate this command with the action of following you before you even begin teaching him to heel.

There is a very precise procedure for teaching your dog to heel. As with all other obedience training, begin with the dog on your left side. He will be in a very nice sit and you will have the training leash across your chest. Hold the loop and folded leash in your right hand. Pick up the slack leash above the dog in your left hand and hold it loosely at your side. Step out on your left foot as you say "Heel." If the puppy does not move, give a gentle tug or pat your left leg to get him started. If he surges ahead of you, stop and pull him back gently until he is at your side. Tell him to sit and begin again.

Walk a few steps and stop while the puppy is correctly beside you. Tell him to sit and give mild verbal praise. (More enthusiastic praise will encourage him to think the lesson is over.) Repeat the lesson, increasing the number of steps you take only as long as the dog is heeling nicely beside you. When you end the lesson, have him hold the sit, then give him the "Okay" to let him know that this is the end of the lesson. Praise him so that he knows he did a good job.

The cure for excessive pulling (a common problem) is to stop when the dog is no more than 2 or

LET'S GO!

Many people use "Let's go" instead of "Heel" when teaching their dogs to behave on lead. It sounds more like fun! When beginning to teach the heel, whatever command you use, always step off on your left foot. That's the one next to the dog, who is on your left side, in case you've forgotten. Keep a loose leash. When the dog pulls ahead, stop, bring him back and begin again. Use treats to guide him around turns.

TRAINING FOR OTHER ACTIVITIES

Once your dog has basic obedience under his collar and is 12 months of age, you may want to begin training for a Canine Good Citizen® title. For those who like to volunteer, there is the wonderful feeling of owning a therapy dog and visiting hospices, nursing homes and veterans' homes to bring smiles, comfort and companionship to those who live there; Komondors are very good at this. Koms are also good at tracking, which is open to all "nosey" dogs.

Around the house, your Komondor can be taught to do some simple chores. You might teach him to carry a small basket of household items or to fetch the morning newspaper. The kids can teach the dog all kinds of tricks, from playing hide-and-seek to balancing a biscuit on his nose. A family dog is what rounds out the family. Everything he does, including sitting at your feet and gazing lovingly at you, represents the bonus of owning a dog.

3 feet ahead of you. Guide him back into position and begin again. With a really determined puller, try quickly turning around and walking the other way. He will be surprised and will stay closer to you. Give quiet, reassuring praise every time the leash goes slack and he's staying with you.

Staying and heeling can take a lot out of a dog, so provide playtime and free-running exercise to shake off the stress when the lessons are over. You don't want him to associate training with all work and no fun.

TAPERING OFF TIDBITS

As you train your Komondor, be wary of being too generous with treats. Even though treats are effective with this breed, it's very easy to overdo it. Your dog has been watching you—and the hand that treats—throughout all of his lessons, and now it's time to break the treat habit. Begin by giving him treats at the end of each lesson only. Then start to give a treat at the end of only some of the lessons. At the end of every lesson, as well as during the lessons, be consistent with the praise. Your pup now doesn't know whether he'll get a treat or not, but he should keep performing well just in case! Finally, you will stop giving treat rewards entirely. Save them for something brand-new that you want to teach him. Keep up the praise and you'll always have a "good dog."

OBEDIENCE CLASSES

The advantages of an obedience class are that your dog will have to learn amid the distractions of other people and dogs and that your mistakes will be quickly corrected by the trainer. In selecting a class, be sure that the instructor likes Komondors. If you sense that he has an aversion or even a dislike for your breed, find another class or school. Too often Komondor owners encounter problems with instructors, which is more common than problems with the dogs themselves.

Teaching your Komondor alongside of a knowledgeable, qualified instructor who likes Koms (and other handlers who may have more dog experience than you) is a true plus of the class environment. The instructor and other handlers can help you to find the most efficient way of teaching your dog a command or exercise. It's often easier to learn by other people's mistakes than your own. You will also learn all of the requirements for competitive obedience trials, in which your Kom can earn titles and go on to advanced jumping and retrieving exercises, which are fun for many dogs. Obedience classes build the foundation needed for many other canine activities (in which we humans are allowed to participate, too!).

ADDITIONAL ADVICE FOR KOMONDOR OWNERS

As a flock guardian, predator control is the Komondor's original task. However, few dogs work well for owners who are not "good with dogs," and the Komondor is not likely to be at his best unless he is trained specifically for his task. No matter how much training, if any, he has had before you get him, in the end how well he performs for you in your situation will depend on how well you have taught him what you require of him.

A Komondor is not a hunting dog, and he is not primarily a herding dog, though on occasion he does herd. He falls into the category of guard dog; originally he was a livestock guard dog and he now is used also to guard people and property. He has no "inborn instincts" to kill predators. He has rather a very strong instinct to protect anything he has come to think of or been

Initially, treats are the best way to motivate your Komondor into following your commands, but eventually you'll want him to respond to all commands consistently without your having to give him the tasty reward.

KOMONDOR

> **TRAINING TIPS FOR KOM OWNERS**
>
> Komondor owners should beware the obedience trainer who thinks livestock dogs are difficult. If your young Komondor is a bit shy around strangers, trainers may tell you that he will be a fear biter. This is probably not so. Youngsters are often very sensitive and perceptive: they react badly to people who dislike them on sight. Avoid excessive training with food. We dislike the present fad for clicker training, not having seen much success with this method on Koms. And do remember that training a Komondor or any livestock guard for work with livestock may well require different methods.

You want your Komondor to come to you enthusiastically when he hears your call.

trained to think of as "his" from anyone, any animal or anything that is strange. This instinct is truly bred into the dog and seems to emerge at maturity without any special training. Indeed we caution owners to be aware that a Komondor will probably protect what is "his" from your friends as well as your enemies, unless the dog is carefully introduced by you to new people and new things. With mechanical things, sometimes introductions cannot help much—a Komondor can "attack" a vacuum cleaner, a lawn mower or a train if he has never seen one before, and more than one dog has died loyally trying to protect his family from a "strange" truck, thinking it a threat to loved ones.

In familiar surroundings a Komondor puppy should be outgoing and friendly, but even a very young puppy may be wary when faced with a stranger unless you supervise introductions and reassure him that the stranger you want him to accept is a friend. We have had puppies only one or two weeks old bark at a stranger's footfall. From around 18 months until around 2 years old, many go through a very trying period of testing—this is a period of adolescence during which they feel in need of proving themselves. They want very much to be the boss, and the human master must be the real boss.

We think that a Kom adjusts best to owner and flock if you get a young puppy and raise him with you and your livestock. If you do this, however, you must realize that the little puppy requires a great deal of supervision in his initial encounters with animals. A grown cow or horse can hurt or even kill a little puppy. A young puppy, on the other hand, can hurt a fragile goat just trying to play with it; after all, a 4-month-old Komondor puppy can weigh over 40 pounds! Your supervision must take both of these extremes into account. As a breed, the Komondor is cautious, conservative and stubborn. It is usually not very hard to supervise first encounters, encouraging good behavior as well as discouraging bad behavior. This is better than trying to prevent disasters later on.

Additionally, we strongly recommend routine obedience training as early as possible. Different owners use different commands, but several things are very basic. First are getting the pup to pay attention to the word "No" and leash training. We follow this with the basics: sit, stay, down and, most importantly, come. Remember always that leash training, sit and down are all things that you can "force" the dog to do to get the idea across. Come is not that kind of command. It is, if you will, an "invitation." For that reason, we advise that every time you give this command and the dog obeys—no matter what he was doing before you called him—you always praise him for coming to you. A dog is not a child, and the learning process is not the same.

The guardian and the herder. A Komondor and his fellow countryman, the Puli, have a romp.

You cannot explain later to a dog what the problem was or why you called him to you. With a dog, you must praise for a correct response as well as reprimand for an incorrect response, but you must never greet a dog's coming to you with a reprimand or he will not want to come when called. The come command is very useful for many things, including calling a dog away from something he should not be doing; in this sense, it is also very important for a dog's safety that he responds reliably when you call him.

A Komondor does not hunt out predators, or anything else, and he also is not a herder, so we usually

Your dog will need some guidance to show him the correct positions that correspond to your verbal commands.

encounter less trouble with chasing chickens, etc., than with many other breeds. However, any dog around livestock, especially small stock, must be watched carefully in the beginning. Correct first encounters are crucial if bad habits are to be avoided. If you, as the owner, show the dog that you care for the stock and protect it, this is often enough to convince a Komondor. Praise for gentle, friendly behavior is as important as reprimanding in case of rough play or chasing. The dogs seem to form special attachments to livestock they have overseen from birth. The lambs that are born after you get the Komondor are more precious to him than the ones that were there before he came. Owners often report that their dogs "fall in love" with the new lambs or kids. Your Komondor will want to be near them, and this should be encouraged, though of course you have to oversee it.

In addition to showing your Kom how to make friends, you will have to teach him who the enemy is. Usually an older dog will teach a younger one. If the dog sees you running after something, chasing it off, or if he feels that you dislike something, he will join you. Sometimes the dogs, even very young ones, simply react to evil intent; a burglar, two-footed or four, will usually rouse the ire of even the most inexperienced dog. The Hungarians often trust Koms' judgement so much that they will not let in any stranger whose way the dogs bar. Here in the US we cannot usually work this way. We see more "strangers" every day, even in remote areas, than most European shepherds do and not all of them like dogs! Komondors rarely like people who don't like them; this is something to remember when "strange" workmen or delivery men arrive. You really need a place where you can confine the dog if someone he does not like must work on or come to your property.

The guarding nature of the breed means usually that few predators are killed. The dogs stay with the flocks and drive predators away. If pressed, the Komondor fights, and he is a formidable fighter. Under ordinary circumstances he will bark and display aggression to announce his presence and forestall forays by predators. Everyone reports that these dogs are quiet by day and bark at night. They also mark their territory with their scent and by scratching the earth. This can mean that often your losses are cut, and your neighbors' losses increase. In view of this, we think it is wise both to introduce the dog to your neighbors and to be sure that your dog learns as quickly as possible what his property boundaries are and that he must not leave his own property. This is the thing that most ranchers report takes the most time and determination.

We wish that everyone could see a Komondor in action before getting one, which is not always possible. The Komondor is not everyone's cup of tea. He requires a firm but affectionate master and works best at maturity if he is considered a fellow shepherd rather than a servant. He is very devoted and hence very sensitive to his owner's displeasure. Physical force is rarely needed (and not recommended) and indeed is sometimes rather sharply resisted if the dog thinks he is being punished when he has no understanding of his "crime." Shaming often works better than physical reprimands.

The Diary of Maggie (for those who have forgotten already) is the diary of a Komondor trained by the Adams family in Evant, Texas to work with their flock of Angora goats. Maggie was a rare animal—even for a Komondor. She was out with that flock in all types of weather, night and day. Not everyone will use a dog the way the Adamses did, but the diary is a valuable aid for anyone training a working dog. In *The Hungarian Komondor*, the writer gives instructions for special care of the dogs and for training them to work with goats. Mrs. Gribble trained four dogs to work with her dairy goat herd; the dogs went out in the morning with the flock, stayed with the flock all day and returned to the barn to sleep with the goats at night. These dogs worked in severe weather in Ontario, Canada, where the predators were wolves. Again, this situation does not pertain to many Komondor owners yet provides a fascinating insight into the nature and the potential of the breed.

Praise and petting are a big part of forming a bond with your dog and rewarding him for appropriate behavior.

PHYSICAL STRUCTURE OF THE KOMONDOR

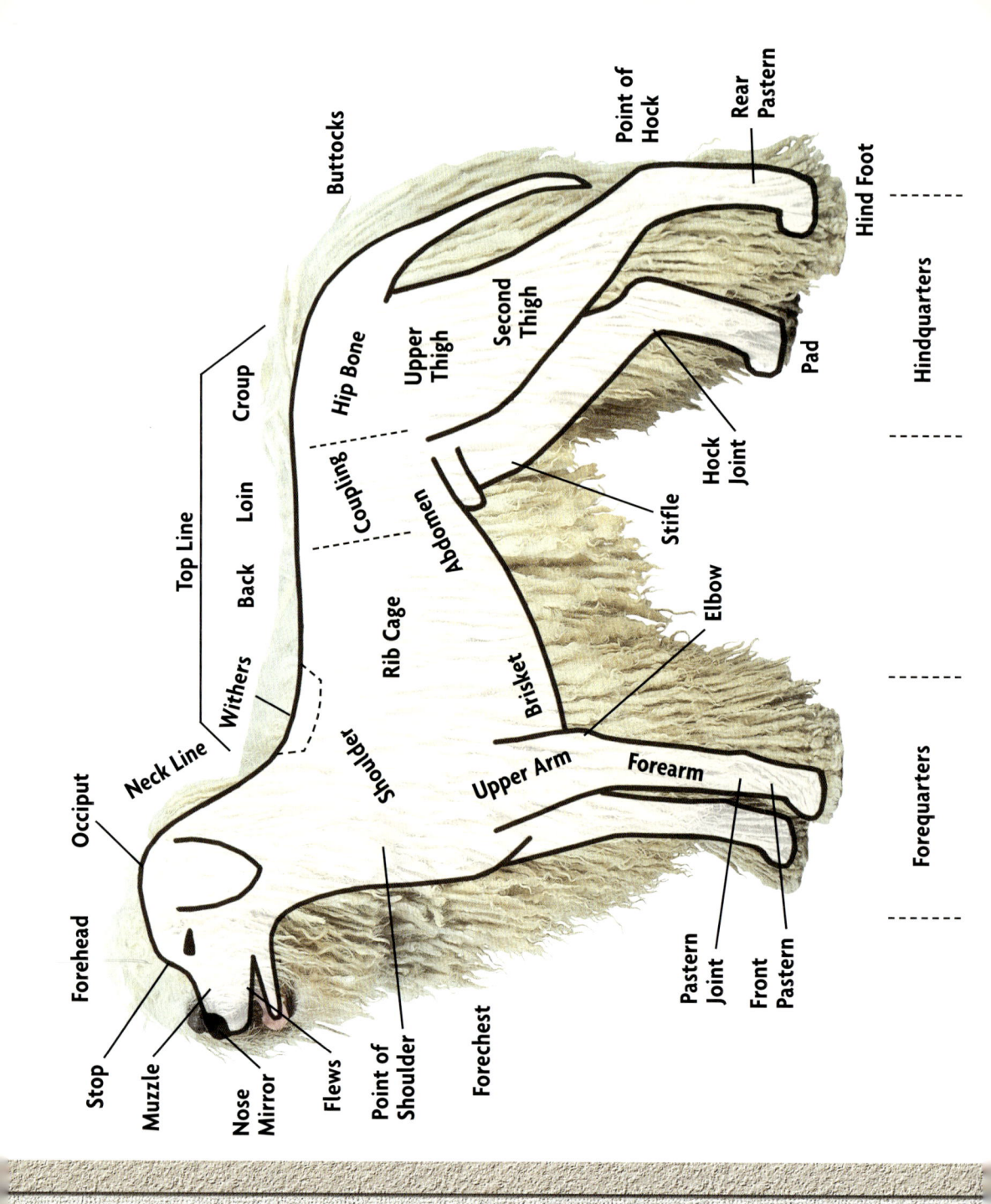

HEALTHCARE OF YOUR

KOMONDOR

By Lowell Ackerman DVM, DACVD

HEALTHCARE FOR A LIFETIME
When you own a dog, you become his healthcare advocate over his entire lifespan, as well as being the one to shoulder the financial burden of such care. Accordingly, it is worthwhile to focus on prevention rather than treatment, as you and your pet will both be happier.

Of course, the best place to have begun your program of preventive healthcare is with the initial purchase or adoption of your dog. There is no way of guaranteeing that your new furry friend is free of medical problems, but there are some things you can do to improve your odds. You certainly should have done adequate research into the Komondor and have selected your puppy carefully rather than buying on impulse. Health issues aside, a large number of pet abandonment and relinquishment cases arise from a mismatch between pet needs and owner expectations. This is entirely preventable with appropriate planning and finding a good breeder.

Regarding healthcare issues specifically, it is very difficult to make blanket statements about where to acquire a problem-free pet, but, again, a reputable breeder is your best bet. In an ideal situation you have the opportunity to see both parents, get references from other owners of the breeder's pups and see genetic-testing documentation for several generations of the litter's ancestors. At the very least, you must thoroughly investigate the Komondor and the problems inherent in that breed, as well as the genetic testing available to screen for those problems. Genetic testing offers some important benefits, but is available for only a few disorders in a relatively small number of breeds and is not available for some of the most common genetic diseases, such as hip dysplasia, cataracts, epilepsy, cardiomyopathy, etc. This area of research is indeed exciting and increasingly important, and advances will continue to be made each year. In fact, recent research has shown that there is an equivalent dog gene for 75% of known human genes, so research done in either species is likely to benefit the other.

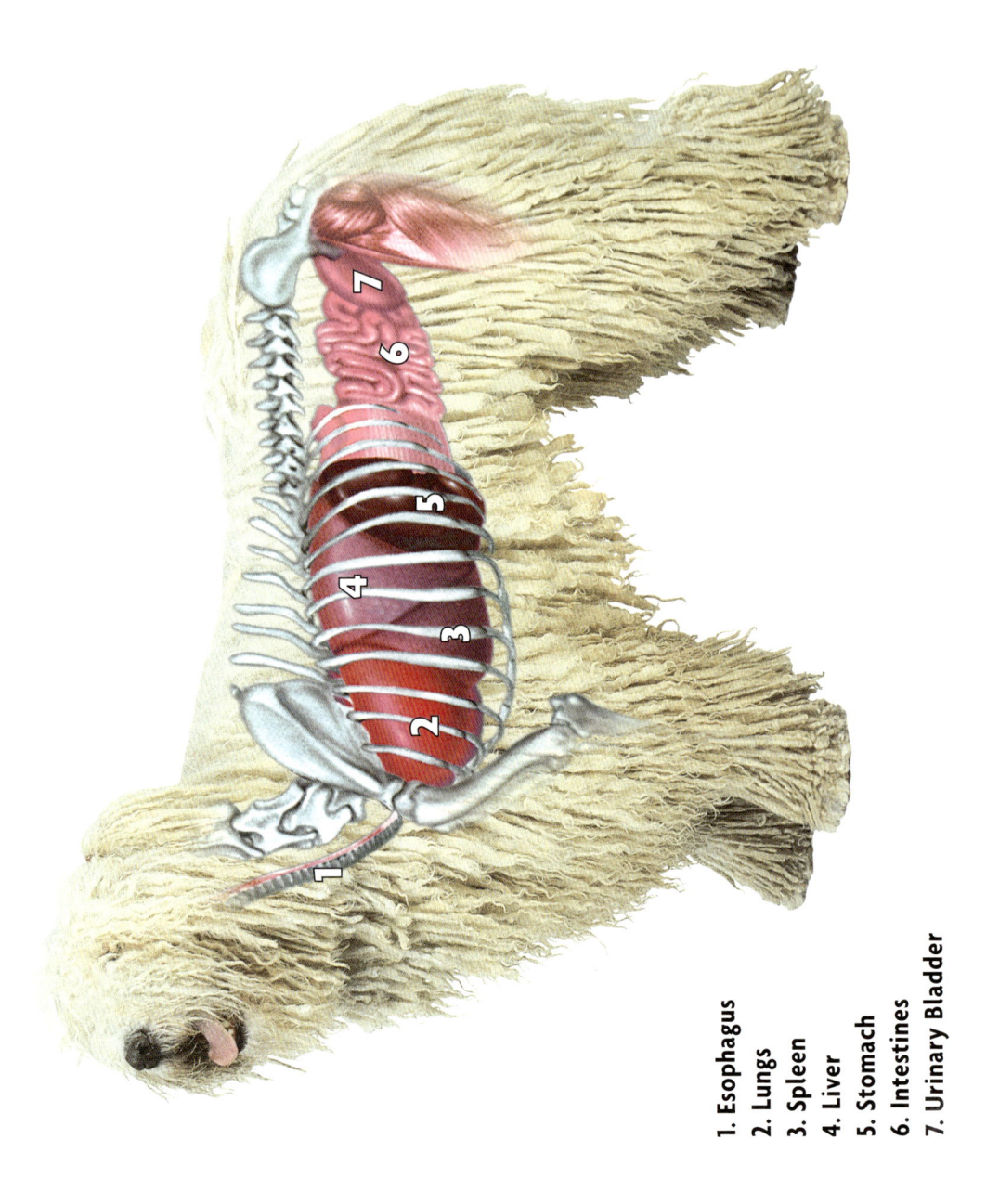

1. Esophagus
2. Lungs
3. Spleen
4. Liver
5. Stomach
6. Intestines
7. Urinary Bladder

INTERNAL ORGANS OF THE KOMONDOR

Healthcare

We've also discussed that evaluating the behavioral nature of your Komondor and that of his immediate family members is an important part of the selection process that cannot be overemphasized. It is sometimes difficult to evaluate temperament in puppies because certain behavioral tendencies, such as some forms of aggression, may not be immediately evident. More dogs are euthanized each year for behavioral reasons than for all medical conditions combined, so it is critical to take temperament issues seriously. Start with a well-balanced, friendly companion and put the time and effort into proper socialization, and you will both be rewarded with a valued relationship.

Assuming that you have started off with a pup from healthy, sound stock, you then become responsible for helping your veterinarian keep your pet healthy. Some crucial things happen before you even bring your puppy home. Parasite control typically begins at two weeks of age, and vaccinations typically begin at six to eight weeks of age. A pre-pubertal evaluation is typically scheduled for about six months of age. At this time, a dental evaluation is done (since the adult teeth are now in), heartworm prevention is started and neutering or spaying can be done.

It is critical to commence regular dental care at home if you have not already done so. It may

> **TAKING YOUR DOG'S TEMPERATURE**
> We have called the vet when a dog seems lethargic, and always the first thing he asks is, "Have you taken his temperature?" Remember that a dog's normal temperature is between 101 and 102 degrees Fahrenheit. We do not worry unless it goes over 103 degrees. Take the temperature rectally, and we recommend a thermometer that has a ring on the end of it. Put a string through this ring and tie a rather long loop on it, so you can shake the thermometer down by twirling it by the string instead of holding it (which I find hard to do). This string is also invaluable in the rare case that a dog retracts the thermometer into his anus. Don't laugh; this can happen, and if you have the string you can (gently) pull the thermometer out again. If your dog seems sick, it is best to take his temperature before you call the vet; it will save everyone valuable time.

not sound very important, but most dogs have active periodontal disease by four years of age if they don't have their teeth cleaned regularly at home, not just at their veterinary exams. Dental problems lead to more than just bad "doggy breath." Gum disease can have very serious medical consequences. If you start brushing your dog's teeth and using antiseptic rinses from a young age, your dog will be accustomed to it and will not

SKELETAL STRUCTURE OF THE KOMONDOR

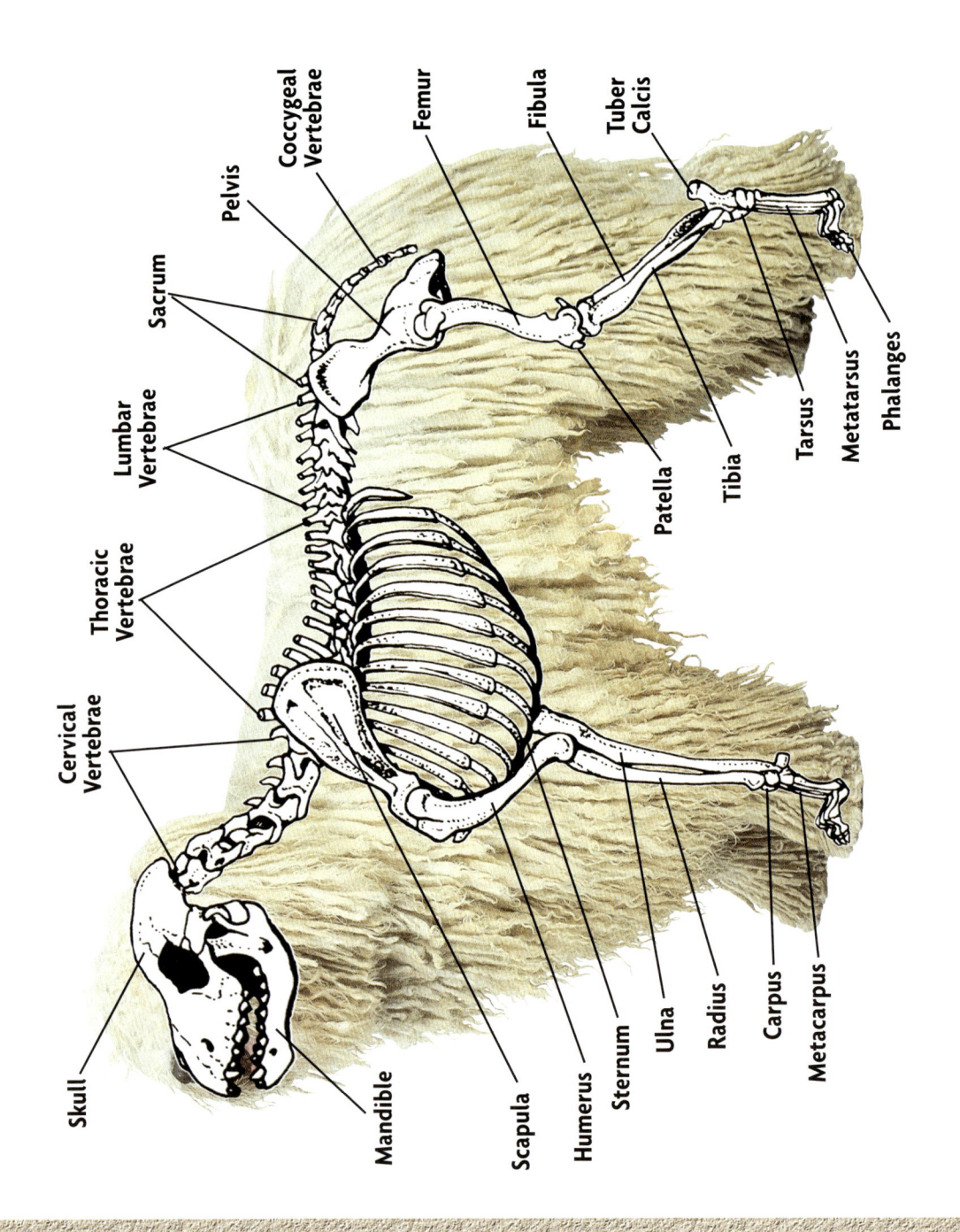

resist. The results will be healthy dentition, which your pet will need to enjoy a long, healthy life.

While many dogs are considered adults at one year of age, larger breeds like the Komondor still have some filling out to do up to about two or so years old. Even individual dogs within each breed have different healthcare requirements, so work with your veterinarian to determine what will be needed and what your role should be. This doctor-client relationship is important, because as vaccination guidelines change, there may not be an annual "vaccine visit" scheduled. You must make sure that you see your veterinarian at least annually, even if no vaccines are due, because this is the best opportunity to coordinate healthcare activities and to make sure that no medical issues creep by unaddressed.

When your Komondor reaches three-quarters of his anticipated lifespan, he is considered a "senior" and likely requires some special care. In general, if you've been taking great care of your canine companion throughout his formative and adult years, the transition to senior status should be a smooth one. Age is not a disease, and as long as everything is functioning as it should, there is no reason why most of late adulthood should not be rewarding for both you and your pet. This is especially true if you have tended to the details, such as regular veterinary visits, proper dental care, excellent nutrition and management of bone and joint issues.

At this stage in your Komondor's life, your veterinarian may want to schedule visits twice yearly, instead of once, to run some laboratory screenings, electrocardiograms and the like, and to change the diet to something more digestible. Catching problems early

SKIN PROBLEMS
Skin problems in the Komondor can vary. Benign cysts are common in older dogs; despite that many cysts are not malignant, any cysts should always be reported and checked by your vet. Komondors also can be susceptible to allergies, whether to food, products in the home, pollen, etc. Sarcoptic mange can also cause an itchy problem. It is important that you keep an eye on your Komondor's skin. Make regular skin checks part of your routine, as abnormalities can easily hide beneath the Komondor's cords.

is the best way to manage them effectively. Treating the early stages of heart disease is so much easier than trying to intervene when there is more significant damage to the heart muscle. Similarly, managing the beginning of kidney problems is fairly routine if there is no significant kidney damage. Other problems, like cognitive dysfunction (similar to senility and Alzheimer's disease), cancer, diabetes and arthritis, are more common in older dogs, but all can be treated to help the dog live as many happy, comfortable years as possible. Just as in people, medical management is more effective (and less expensive) when you catch things early.

SELECTING A VETERINARIAN
There is probably no more important decision that you will make regarding your pet's healthcare than the selection of his doctor. Your pet's veterinarian will be a pediatrician, family-practice physician and gerontologist, depending on the dog's life stage, and will be the individual who makes recommendations regarding issues such as when specialists need to be consulted, when diagnostic testing and/or therapeutic intervention is needed and when you will need to seek outside emergency and critical-care services. Your vet will act as your advocate and liaison throughout these processes.

For the Komondor, you have several considerations. You want a vet who has experience in the breed, as they will be familiar with its special health issues and temperament. If you cannot find a vet who knows the Komondor, you at least want one who is not intimidated by the breed and is willing to work with you. A Komondor's vet must always keep in mind the breed's sensitivity to anesthesia and to certain parasite preventives and other medications. If you cannot be recommended to a vet for your Komondor, you will have to talk to the vets in your area to find the best choice.

Everyone has his own idea about what to look for in a vet, an individual who will play a big role in his dog's (and, of course, his own) life for many years to come. For some, it is the compassionate caregiver with whom they hope to develop a professional relationship to span the lifetime of their dogs and even their future pets. For others, they are seeking a clinician with keen diagnostic and therapeutic insight who can deliver state-of-the-art healthcare. Still others need a veterinary facility that is open evenings and weekends, is in close proximity or provides mobile veterinary services to accommodate their schedules; these people may not mind that their dogs might see different veterinarians on each visit. Just as we have different reasons for selecting our own healthcare professionals (e.g., covered by insurance plan, expert in field, convenient location, etc.), we should not expect that there is a one-size-fits-all recommendation for selecting a veterinarian and veterinary practice. The best advice is to be honest in your assessment of what you expect from a veterinary practice and to conscientiously research the options in your area. You will quickly appreciate that not all veterinary practices are the same, and you will be happiest with one that truly meets your needs.

There is another point to be considered in the selection of veterinary services. Not that long ago, a single veterinarian would attempt to manage all medical and surgical issues as they arose. That was often problematic, because veterinarians are trained in many species and many diseases, and it was just impossible for general veterinary practitioners to be experts in every species, every breed, every field and every ailment. However, just as in the human healthcare fields, specialization has allowed general practitioners to concentrate on primary healthcare delivery, especially wellness and the prevention of infectious diseases, and to utilize a network of specialists to assist in the management of conditions that require specific expertise and experience. Thus there are now many types of veterinary specialists, including dermatologists, cardiologists, ophthalmologists, surgeons, internists, oncologists, neurologists, behaviorists, criticalists and others to help primary-care veterinarians deal with complicated medical challenges. In most cases, specialists see cases referred by primary-care veterinarians, make diagnoses and set up management plans. From there, the animals' ongoing care is returned to their primary-care veterinarians. This important team approach to your pet's medical-care needs has provided opportunities for advanced care and an unparalleled level of quality to be delivered.

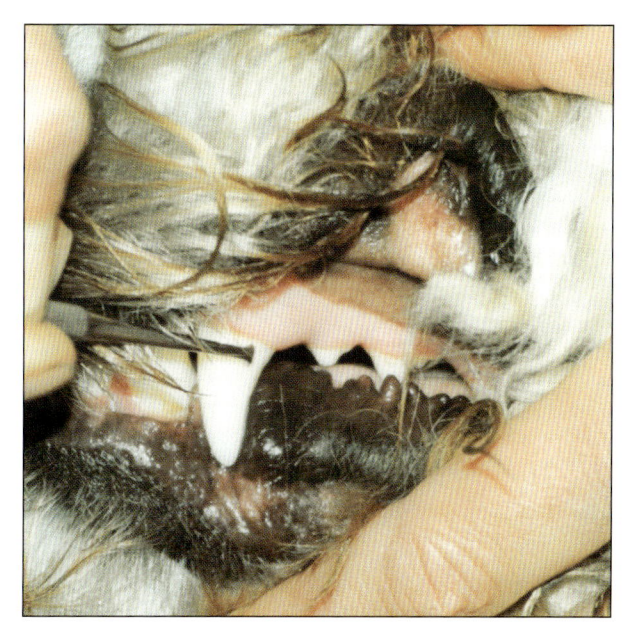

With all of the opportunities for your Komondor to receive high-quality veterinary medical care, there is another topic that needs to be addressed at the same time—cost. It's been said that you can have excellent healthcare or inexpensive healthcare, but never both; this is as true in veterinary medicine as it is in human medicine. While veterinary costs are a fraction of what the same

Paying attention to your dog's teeth is an essential facet of his proper healthcare. Many serious problems can stem from a lack of effective dental care.

services cost in the human healthcare arena, it is still difficult to deal with unanticipated medical costs, especially since they can easily creep into hundreds or even thousands of dollars if specialists or emergency services become involved. However, there are ways of managing these risks. The easiest is to buy pet health insurance and realize that its foremost purpose is not to cover routine healthcare visits but rather to serve as an umbrella for those rainy days when your pet needs medical care and you don't want to worry about whether or not you can afford that care.

Pet insurance policies are very cost-effective (and very inexpensive by human health-insurance standards), but make sure that you buy the policy long before you intend to use it (preferably starting in puppyhood, because coverage will exclude pre-existing conditions) and that you are actually buying an indemnity insurance plan from an insurance company that is regulated by your state or province. Many insurance policy look-alikes are actually discount clubs that are redeemable only at specific locations and for specific services. An indemnity plan covers your pet at almost all veterinary, specialty and emergency practices and is an excellent way to manage your pet's ongoing healthcare needs.

VACCINATIONS AND INFECTIOUS DISEASES

There has never been an easier time to prevent a variety of infectious diseases in your dog, but the advances we've made in veterinary medicine come with a price—choice. Now while it may seem that choice regarding your pet's vaccinations is a good thing (and it is), it also has never been more difficult for the pet owner (or the veterinarian) to make an informed decision about the best way to protect pets through vaccination.

Years ago, it was just accepted that puppies got a starter series of vaccinations and then annual "boosters" throughout their lives to keep them protected. As more and more vaccines became available, consumers wanted the convenience of having all of that protection in a single injection. The result was "multivalent" vaccines that crammed a lot of protection into a single syringe. The manufacturers' recommendations were to give the vaccines annually, and this was a simple enough protocol to follow. However, as veterinary medicine has become more sophisticated and we have started looking more at healthcare quandaries rather than convenience, it became necessary to reevaluate the situation and deal with some tough questions. It is important to realize that whether or not to use a particular vaccine depends on the risk of contracting the disease against which it

Common Infectious Diseases

Let's discuss some of the diseases that create the need for vaccination in the first place. Following are the major canine infectious diseases and a simple explanation of each.

Rabies: A devastating viral disease that can be fatal in dogs and people. In fact, vaccination of dogs and cats is an important public-health measure to create a resistant animal buffer population to protect people from contracting the disease. Vaccination schedules are determined on a government level and are not optional for pet owners; rabies vaccination is required by law in all 50 states.

Parvovirus: A severe, potentially life-threatening disease that is easily transmitted between dogs. There are four strains of the virus, but it is believed that there is significant "cross-protection" between strains that may be included in individual vaccines.

Distemper: A potentially severe and life-threatening disease with a relatively high risk of exposure, especially in certain regions. In very high-risk distemper environments, young pups may be vaccinated with human measles vaccine, a related virus that offers cross-protection when administered at four to ten weeks of age.

Hepatitis: Caused by canine adenovirus type 1 (CAV-1), but since vaccination with the causative virus has a higher rate of adverse effects, cross-protection is derived from the use of adenovirus type 2 (CAV-2), a cause of respiratory disease and one of the potential causes of canine cough. Vaccination with CAV-2 provides long-term immunity against hepatitis, but relatively less protection against respiratory infection.

Canine cough: Also called tracheobronchitis, actually a fairly complicated result of viral and bacterial offenders; therefore, even with vaccination, protection is incomplete. Wherever dogs congregate, canine cough will likely be spread among them. Intranasal vaccination with *Bordetella* and parainfluenza is the best safeguard, but the duration of immunity does not appear to be very long, typically a year at most. These are non-core vaccines, but vaccination is sometimes mandated by boarding kennels, obedience classes, dog shows and other places where dogs congregate to try to minimize spread of infection.

Leptospirosis: A potentially fatal disease that is more common in some geographic regions. It is capable of being spread to humans. The disease varies with the individual "serovar," or strain, of *Leptospira* involved. Since there does not appear to be much cross-protection between serovars, protection is only as good as the likelihood that the serovar in the vaccine is the same as the one in the pet's local environment. Problems with *Leptospira* vaccines are that protection does not last very long, side effects are not uncommon and a large percentage of dogs (perhaps 30%) may not respond to vaccination.

Borrelia burgdorferi: The cause of Lyme disease, the risk of which varies with the geographic area in which the pet lives and travels. Lyme disease is spread by deer ticks in the eastern US and western black-legged ticks in the western part of the country, and the risk of exposure is high in some regions. Lameness, fever and inappetence are most commonly seen in affected dogs. The extent of protection from the vaccine has not been conclusively demonstrated.

Coronavirus: This disease has a high risk of exposure, especially in areas where dogs congregate, but it typically causes only mild to moderate digestive upset (diarrhea, vomiting, etc.). Vaccines are available, but the duration of protection is believed to be relatively short and the effectiveness of the vaccine in preventing infection is considered low.

There are many other vaccinations available, including those for *Giardia* and canine adenovirus-1. While there may be some specific indications for their use, and local risk factors to be considered, they are not widely recommended for most dogs.

Vaccinations are just one of the avenues that help to keep your Kom free from disease.

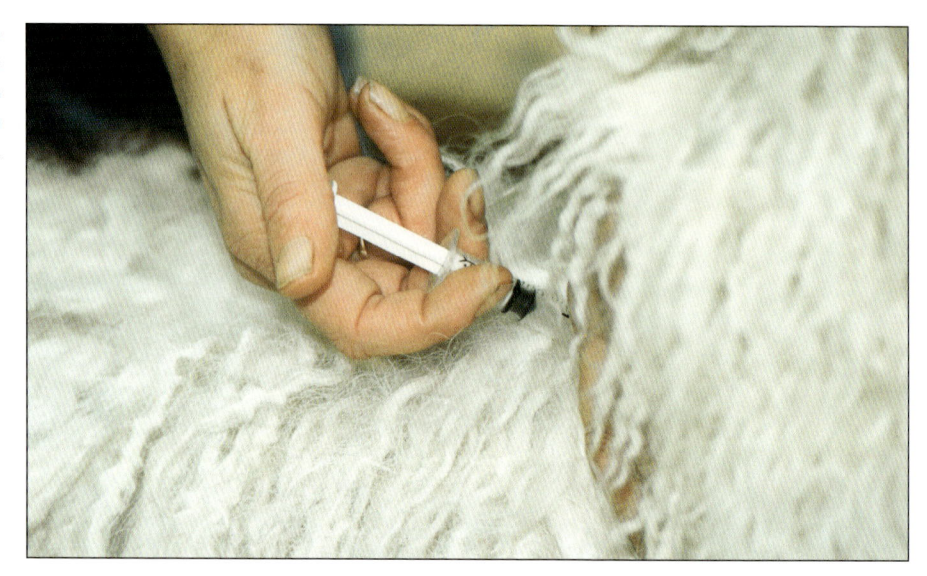

protects, the severity of the disease if it is contracted, the duration of immunity provided by the vaccine, the safety of the product and the needs of the individual animal.

When you bring your Komondor puppy home, he will come with a record of his vaccinations up to that point. The breeder follows his vet's advice for vaccinating the puppies, but your vet may prefer a different schedule. I recommend doing what your vet says to do. Puppies are regularly vaccinated for distemper, parvovirus, hepatitis and respiratory disease. They also get a first rabies vaccination at around four months of age and this lasts only one year. After a rabies booster at one year, dogs then typically get a rabies vaccine every three years (although this depends on the regulations in your locality).

Some years ago, vets all gave the leptospirosis vaccine in the first combined shots. Many vets no longer do this, partly because they feel it is unnecessary and partly because some dogs react adversely to the leptospirosis component. If a leptospirosis vaccine is given, it is usually given separately. Vets differ in opinion about giving vaccines for Lyme disease, *Giardia* and kennel cough (usually *Bordetella*); these vaccines are usually given or not given based on where a dog lives and his individual risk of exposure. Some vets recommend the coronavirus vaccine for dogs, especially those being shown or exercised around a lot of other dogs.

Recently a lot has been written

about yearly booster shots. We don't booster our dogs yearly after a certain age. I don't give boosters to old dogs for anything but rabies, which is required in every state before you can get a dog license (usually required every three years). I also do not give a booster shot to bitches I expect to breed until they have weaned their litter. If you give a bitch a booster shot just before she has a litter, this may raise the titer (antibody level) for puppies so high that their puppy shots will not be effective.

SPAYING AND NEUTERING
The common belief is that bitches should be spayed young or else they will get breast cancer. This is not a hard and fast truth; they might or might not. We do not approve of spaying bitches at too young an age; the average age for a Komondor's first heat is one year. Animals altered too young seem to us never to mature properly. This means that pet Komondor owners must be very responsible with their bitches until the proper age for spaying is reached. If for some reason a bitch has to change owners before she is spayed, care must be taken to ensure that she does not go to someone with plans to breed her irresponsibly. The new owner must be responsible and must have her spayed at the appropriate age.

As for altering males, if the owner is responsible this is rarely ever necessary unless the vet advises it for medical reasons. If the dog marks the house, it might be an option, but we feel that no responsible owner should have a male Komondor wandering off lead where he can overpopulate the world. In any case, neutering an animal who has recently been relocated is a bad idea; it is much better to have him well settled and used to a new owner and new surroundings. One dog recently came home after neutering and didn't seem right. By the next day, he went into gastric dilatation/volvulus bloat. It seems to me that something put too much strain on his system. Having an unneutered male does require vigilance on the owner's part that he is not allowed to mate and that he does not fall into the hands of someone with irresponsible intentions.

> **DENTAL WARNING SIGNS**
> A veterinary dental exam is necessary if you notice one or any combination of the following in your dog:
> - Broken, loose or missing teeth
> - Loss of appetite (which could be due to mouth pain or illness caused by infection)
> - Gum abnormalities, including redness, swelling and bleeding
> - Drooling, with or without blood
> - Yellowing of the teeth or gumline, indicating tartar
> - Bad breath.

A scanning electron micrograph of a dog flea, *Ctenocephalides canis*, on dog hair.

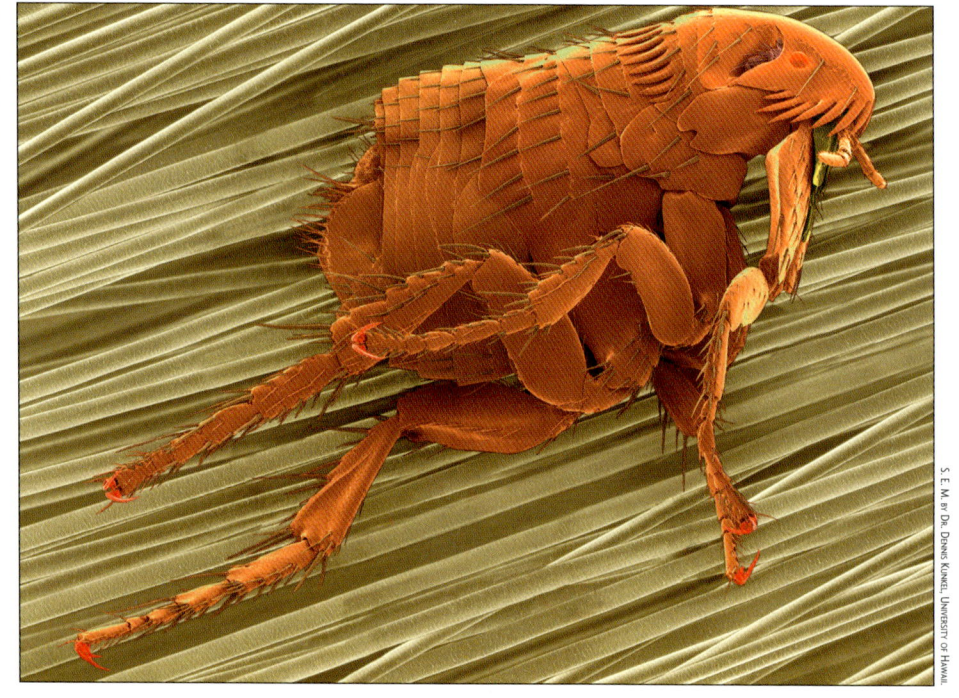

EXTERNAL PARASITES

FLEAS

Fleas have been around for millions of years and, while we have better tools now for controlling them than at any time in the past, there still is little chance that they will end up on an endangered species list. Actually, they are very well adapted to living on our pets, and they continue to adapt as we make advances.

The female flea can consume 15 times her weight in blood during active reproduction and can lay as many as 40 eggs a day. These eggs are very resistant to the effects of insecticides. They hatch into larvae, which then mature and spin cocoons. The immature fleas reside in this pupal stage until the time is right for feeding. This pupal stage is also very resistant to the effects of insecticides, and pupae can last in the environment without feeding for many months. Newly emergent fleas are attracted to animals by the warmth of the animals' bodies, movement and exhaled carbon dioxide. However, when they first emerge from their cocoons, they orient towards light; thus when an animal passes between a flea and the light source, casting a shadow, the flea pounces and starts to feed. If the animal turns out to be a dog or cat, the reproductive cycle

Healthcare

continues. If the flea lands on another type of animal, including a person, the flea will bite but will then look for a more appropriate host. An emerging adult flea can survive without feeding for up to 12 months but, once it tastes blood, it can only survive off its host for 3–4 days.

It was once thought that fleas spend most of their lives in the environment, but we now know that fleas won't willingly jump off a dog unless leaping to another dog or when physically removed by brushing, bathing or other manipulation. Flea eggs, on the other hand, are shiny and smooth, and they roll off the animal and into the environment. The eggs, larvae and pupae then exist in the environment, but once the adult finds a susceptible animal, it's home sweet home until the flea is convinced to seek refuge elsewhere.

Since adult fleas live on the animal and immature forms survive in the environment, a successful treatment plan must address all stages of the flea life cycle. There are now several safe and effective flea-control products that can be applied on a monthly basis. Most of these products have significant flea-killing rates within 24 hours. However, none of them will control the immature forms in the environment. To accomplish this, there are a variety of insect growth regulators that can be sprayed into the environment as well as insect development inhibitors that can be administered. These compounds have no effect on adult fleas, but they stop immature forms from developing into adults.

Discuss your Komondor's sensitivity to parasite preventives with your breeder and vet to help put together a safe way to protect your dog. Komondors (and similar breeds) are very susceptible to these products and it may not be advised to combine more than one anti-flea chemical. Further, a flea preventive may cause a reaction in conjunction with a heartworm or other parasite preventive. Prepara-

PARASITE PREVENTIVES
Owners must be warned that Komondors (and other livestock guard dogs) are very susceptible to anti-flea preparations. Administer any flea sprays or dips with great caution, remembering that a great deal more stays on a Komondor's coat than on the coat of a short- or smooth-haired dog. Overdosing or allergic reactions may cause convulsions, which can have serious consequences. If you have your dog on year-round heartworm preventives, as many of us do, remember that this is being combined with whatever anti-flea poison you are administering. If you have sprayed your yard or fogged your house, this too will affect your dog. Combining several poisons can have unexpected consequences; for example, a flea dip combined with a flea collar can have bad results. Think and check with your veterinarian. You must be careful in administering any worming medications or preparations for controlling fleas or ticks.

THE FLEA'S LIFE CYCLE

What came first, the flea or the egg? This age-old mystery is more difficult to comprehend than the actual cycle of the flea. Fleas usually live only about four months. A female can lay 2,000 eggs in her lifetime.

Egg

After ten days of rolling around your carpet or under your furniture, the eggs hatch into larvae, which feed on various and sundry debris. In days or months, depending on the climate, the larvae spin cocoons and develop into the pupal or nymph stage, which quickly develop into fleas.

Larva

Pupa

These immature fleas must locate a host within 10 to 14 days or they will die. Only about 1% of the flea population exist as adult fleas, while the other 99% exist as eggs, larvae or pupae.

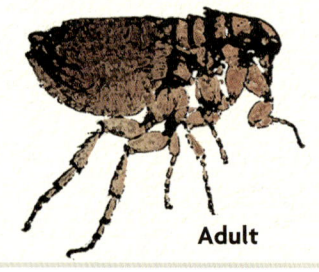

Adult

KILL FLEAS THE NATURAL WAY

If you choose not to go the route of conventional medication, there are some natural ways to ward off fleas:
- Dust your dog with a natural flea powder, composed of such herbal goodies as rosemary, wormwood, pennyroyal, citronella, rue, tobacco powder and eucalyptus.
- Apply diatomaceous earth, the fossilized remains of single-cell algae, to your carpets, furniture and pet's bedding. Even though it's not good for dogs, it's even worse for fleas, which will dry up swiftly and die.
- Check your dog's coat frequently, give him adequate exercise and let him fast occasionally. All of these activities strengthen the dog's immune system and make him more resistant to disease and parasites.
- Bathe your dog with a capful of pennyroyal or eucalyptus oil.
- Feed a natural diet, free of additives and preservatives. Add a little fresh garlic and brewer's yeast to the dog's morning portion, as these items have flea-repelling properties.

tions such as sprays or dips can be dangerous as the Komondor's coat absorbs and retains higher quantities of the product than shorter-coated dogs. You must be careful in administering all parasite-control preparations to your Komondor, as overdosing can cause very serious consequences.

TICKS

Ticks are members of the spider class (arachnids) and are blood-sucking parasites capable of transmitting a variety of diseases, including Lyme disease, ehrlichiosis, babesiosis and Rocky Mountain spotted fever. It's easy to see ticks on your own skin, but it is

Healthcare

more of a challenge when your furry companion is affected. Whenever you happen to be planning a stroll in a tick-infested area (especially forests, grassy or wooded areas or parks) be prepared to do a thorough inspection of your dog afterward to search for ticks. Ticks can be tricky, so make sure you spend time looking in the ears, between the toes and everywhere else a tick might hide. Ticks need to be attached for 24–72 hours before they transmit most of the diseases that they carry, so you do have a window of opportunity for some preventive intervention.

Female ticks live to eat and breed. They can lay between 4,000 and 5,000 eggs and they die soon after. Males, on the other hand, live on to mate and continue the process as long as they are able. Most ticks live on multiple hosts before parasitizing dogs. The immature forms typically reside on grass and shrubs, waiting for susceptible animals to walk by. The larvae and nymph stages typically feed on wildlife.

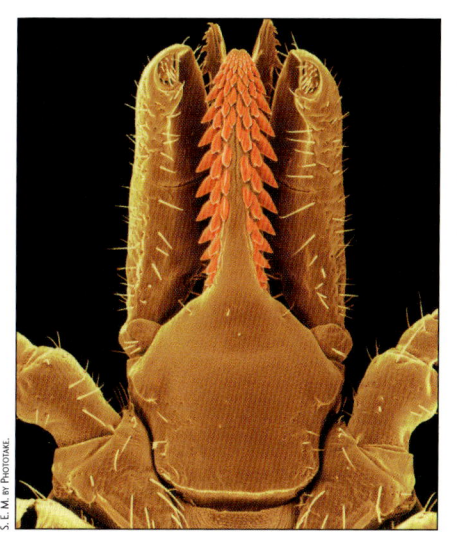

If only a few ticks are present on a dog, they can be plucked out, but it is important to remove the entire head and mouthparts, which may be deeply embedded in the skin. This is best accomplished with forceps designed especially for this purpose; fingers can be used but should be protected with rubber gloves, plastic wrap or at least a paper towel. The tick should be grasped as closely as possible to the animal's skin and should be pulled upward with steady, even pressure. Do not squeeze, crush or puncture the body of the tick or you risk exposure to any disease carried by that tick. Once the ticks have been removed, the sites of attachment should be disinfected. The hands should then be washed with soap and water to further minimize risk of contagion.

A scanning electron micrograph of the head of a female deer tick, *Ixodes dammini*, a parasitic tick that carries Lyme disease.

A TICKING BOMB

There is nothing good about a tick's harpooning his nose into your dog's skin. Among the diseases caused by ticks are Rocky Mountain spotted fever, canine ehrlichiosis, canine babesiosis, canine hepatozoonosis and Lyme disease. If a dog is allergic to the saliva of a female wood tick, he can develop tick paralysis.

Deer tick, Ixodes dammini.

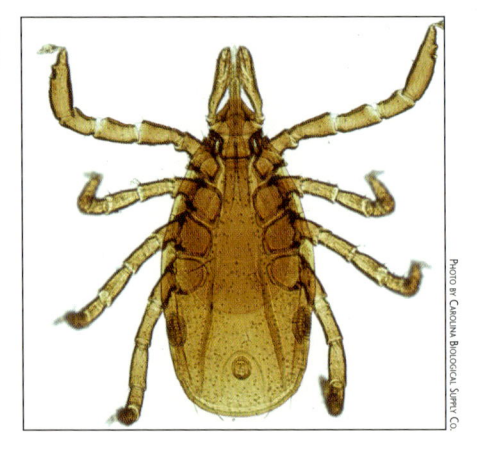

The tick should be disposed of in a container of alcohol or flushed down the toilet.

Removal of underbrush and leaf litter and the thinning of trees in areas where tick control is desired are recommended. These actions remove the cover and food sources for small animals that serve as hosts for ticks. With continued mowing of grasses in these areas, the probability of ticks' surviving is further reduced.

Discuss the Lyme disease vaccine with your vet; some recommend it and others do not. Lyme disease is found in just about every state; there is a vaccine now for humans, too. Not every dog that limps is dysplastic; limping is also a symptom of Lyme disease. Other symptoms can be joint pain that seems to affect different joints at different times, lethargy and general poor condition. If the vet suspects Lyme disease, early administration of antibiotics is given, whether a test is positive or not. Lyme disease tests are not always reliable.

As for prevention, it can be difficult in some parts of the country. Dips can be ineffective; flea and tick collars for dogs that are outside in known tick-infested areas are more successful, but vigilance is the real answer. We have had good results with collars containing amitraz. These have not kept the dogs completely tick-free but have greatly reduced the number of ticks we find on them. Several Komondor owners have reported good results with the medication that is applied every three or four months to the dog's neck. No matter what you use, check your dog often for fleas and

Sarcoptes scabiei, commonly known as the "itch mite."

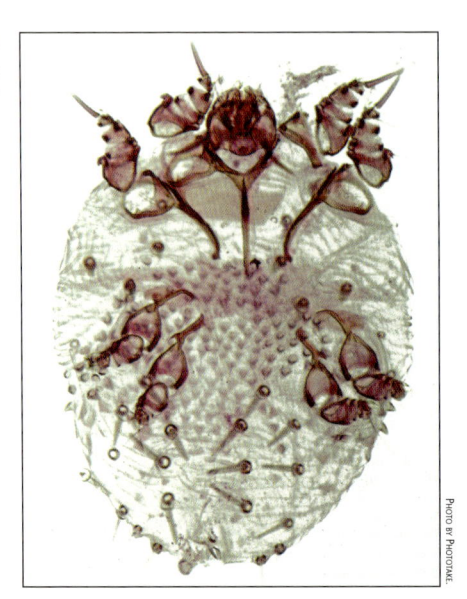

Healthcare

LYME DISEASE

Lyme disease, first observed in Lyme, Connecticut in 1977, is transmitted by black-legged ticks (*Ixodes scapularis*) in the northeastern and north-central part of the US and by the western black-legged tick (*Ixodes pacificus*) on the West Coast. The bacterium that causes the disease, *Borrelia burgdorferi*, is transmitted to people by infected deer ticks. Estimates indicate that 20,000-25,000 new cases are reported annually in the US.

Characterized by a bull's-eye rash, Lyme disease presents symptoms such as fever, malaise, fatigue, headache, muscle aches and joint aches. The highly recognizable lesion at the onset of Lyme disease is referred to as erythema migrans, which can occur as soon as 3 days from infection to as long as 30 days later, though the typical time frame is between 7 and 14 days. The disease can manifest itself neurologically (facial nerve palsy, meningitis) or as muscle and joint problems (possible swelling), as well as in heart defects, which are rare.

ticks and remove any promptly. Also keep in mind the breed's sensitivity to parasite preventives and do not overdo it with too many anti-parasite drugs. Discuss safe tick protection with your vet and breeder.

Recently we have had reports of Komondors with ehrlichiosis, also transmitted by ticks. The symptoms are often very similar to those of Lyme disease. If your dog limps, the vet should consider testing for both of these tick-borne diseases. Treatment is the same for both, with doxycycline the drug of choice.

MOSQUITOES

Mosquitoes have long been known to transmit a variety of diseases to people, as well as just being biting pests during warm weather. They also pose a real risk to pets. Not only do they carry deadly heartworms but recently there also has been much concern over their involvement with West Nile virus. While we can avoid heartworm with the use of preventive medications, there are no such preventives for West Nile virus; the only method of prevention in endemic areas is active mosquito control. Fortunately, most dogs that have been exposed to the virus only developed flu-like symptoms and, to date, there have not been the large number of reported deaths in canines as seen in some other species.

Low concentrations of DEET (less than 10%), found in many human mosquito repellents, have been safely used in dogs but, in these concentrations, probably only give about two hours of protection. DEET may be safe in these small concentrations, but since it is not licensed for use on

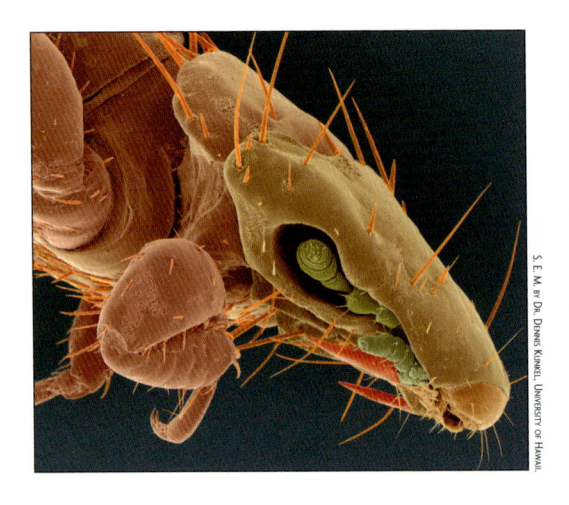

Micrograph of a dog louse, Heterodoxus spiniger. Female lice attach their eggs to the hairs of the dog. As the eggs hatch, the larval lice bite and feed on the blood. Lice can also feed on dead skin and hair. This feeding activity can cause hair loss and skin problems.

dogs, there is no research proving its safety for dogs. Products containing permethrin give the longest-lasting protection, perhaps two to four weeks. As DEET is not licensed for use on dogs, and both DEET and permethrin can be quite toxic to cats, appropriate care should be exercised. Other products, such as those containing oil of citronella, also have some mosquito-repellent activity, but they typically have relatively short duration of action.

MITES

Mites are tiny arachnid parasites that parasitize the skin of dogs. Skin diseases caused by mites are referred to as "mange"; there are many different forms seen in dogs. These forms are very different from one another, each one warranting an individual description.

Sarcoptic mange, or scabies, is one of the itchiest conditions that affects dogs. The microscopic *Sarcoptes* mites burrow into the superficial layers of the skin and can drive dogs crazy with itchiness. They are also communicable to people, although they can't complete their reproductive cycle on people. Not only are the mites tiny but also are often difficult to find when trying to make a diagnosis. Skin scrapings from multiple areas are examined microscopically but, even then, sometimes the mites cannot be found.

Fortunately, scabies is relatively easy to treat, and there are a variety of products that will successfully kill the mites. Since the mites can't live in the environment for very long without feeding, a complete cure is usually possible within four to eight weeks.

Cheyletiellosis is caused by a relatively large mite, which sometimes can be seen even without a microscope. Often referred to as "walking dandruff," this also causes itching, but not usually as profound as with scabies. While *Cheyletiella* mites can survive somewhat longer in the environment than scabies mites, they too are relatively easy to treat, being responsive not only to the medications used to treat scabies but also often to flea-control products.

Otodectes cynotis is the cause of ear mites and is one of the more common causes of mange, especially in young dogs in shelters or pet stores. That's because the mites are typically present in large numbers and are quickly spread to nearby animals. The mites rarely do much harm but can be difficult to eradicate if the treatment regimen is not comprehensive. While many try to treat the condition with ear drops only, this is the most common cause of treatment failure. Ear drops cause the mites to simply move out of the ears and as far away as possible (usually to the base of the tail) until the miticide levels in the ears drop to an acceptable level—then it's back to business as usual! The successful treatment of ear mites requires treating all animals in the household with a systemic insecticide, such as selamectin, or a combination of miticidal ear drops combined with whole-body flea control preparations.

Demodicosis, sometimes referred to as red mange, can be one of the most difficult forms of mange to treat. Part of the problem has to do with the fact that the mites live in the hair follicles and thus are relatively well shielded from topical and systemic products. The main issue, however, is that demodectic mange typically results only when there is some underlying process interfering with the dog's immune system.

Since *Demodex* mites are normal residents of the skin of mammals, including humans, there is usually a mite population explosion only when the immune system fails to keep the number of mites in check. In young animals, the immune deficit may be transient or may reflect an actual inherited immune problem. In older animals, demodicosis is usually seen only when there is another disease hampering the immune system, such as diabetes, cancer, thyroid problems or the use of immune-suppressing drugs. Accordingly, treatment involves not only trying to kill the mange mites but also discerning what is interfering with immune function and correcting it if possible.

Chiggers represent several different species of mite that don't parasitize dogs specifically, but do attach themselves to passersby and can cause irritation. The problem is most prevalent in wooded areas in the late summer and fall. Treatment is not difficult, as the mites do not complete their life cycle on dogs and are susceptible to a variety of miticidal products.

Illustration of *Demodex folliculoram*.

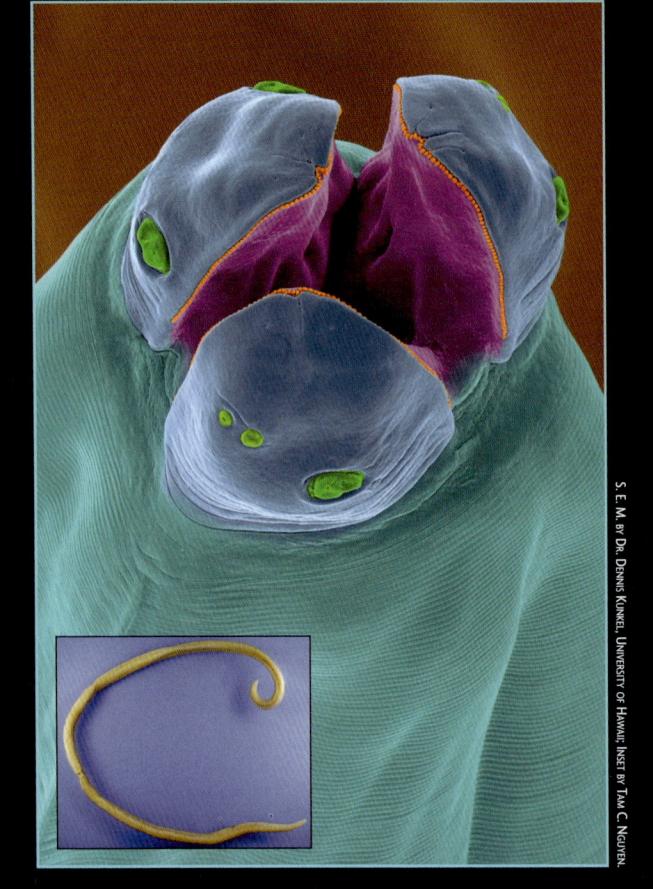

ASCARID DANGERS

The most commonly encountered worms in dogs are roundworms known as ascarids. *Toxascaris leonine* and *Toxocara canis* are the two species that infect dogs. Subsisting in the dog's stomach and intestines, adult roundworms can grow to 7 inches in length and adult females can lay in excess of 200,000 eggs in a single day.

In humans, visceral larval migrans affects people who have ingested eggs of *Toxocara canis*, which frequently contaminates children's sandboxes, beaches and park grounds. The roundworms reside in the human's stomach and intestines, as they would in a dog's, but do not mature. Instead, they find their way to the liver, lungs and skin, or even to the heart or kidneys in severe cases. Deworming puppies is critical in preventing the infection in humans, and young children should never handle nursing pups who have not been dewormed.

The ascarid roundworm Toxocara canis, showing the mouth with three lips. INSET: Photomicrograph of the roundworm Ascaris lumbricoides.

INTERNAL PARASITES: WORMS

ASCARIDS

Ascarids, one family of the nematode (roundworm) group, are intestinal parasites that rarely cause severe disease in dogs. Nonetheless, they are of major public health significance because they can be transferred to people. Sadly, it is children who are most commonly affected with the parasite, probably from inadvertently ingesting ascarid-contaminated soil. In fact, many yards and children's sandboxes contain appreciable numbers of ascarid eggs. So while ascarids don't bite dogs or latch on to their intestines to suck blood, they do cause some nasty medical conditions in children and are best eradicated from our furry friends. Because pups can start passing ascarid eggs by three weeks of age, most parasite-control programs begin at two weeks of age and are repeated every two weeks until pups are

HOOKED ON ANCYLOSTOMA

Adult dogs can become infected by the bloodsucking nematodes we commonly call hookworms via ingesting larvae from the ground or via the larvae penetrating the dog's skin. It is not uncommon for infected dogs to show no symptoms of hookworm infestation. Sometimes symptoms occur within ten days of exposure. These symptoms can include bloody diarrhea, anemia, loss of weight and general weakness. Dogs pass the hookworm eggs in their stools, which serves as the vet's method of identifying the infestation. The hookworm larvae can encyst themselves in the dog's tissues and be released when the dog is experiencing stress.

Caused by an *Ancylostoma* species whose common host is the dog, cutaneous larval migrans affects humans, causing itching and lumps and streaks beneath the surface of the skin.

S.E.M. by Dr. Dennis Kunkel, University of Hawaii.

The hookworm *Ancylostoma caninum* infests the intestines of dogs. INSET: Note the row of hooks at the posterior end, used to anchor the worm to the intestinal wall.

eight weeks old. It is important to realize that bitches can pass ascarids to their pups even if they test negative prior to whelping. Accordingly, bitches are best treated at the same time as the pups.

HOOKWORMS

Unlike ascarids, hookworms do latch on to a dog's intestinal tract and can cause significant loss of blood and protein. Like ascarids, hookworms can be transmitted to humans, where they cause a condition known as cutaneous larval migrans. Dogs can become infected either by consuming the infective larvae or by the larvae's penetrating the skin directly. People most often get infected when they are lying on the ground (such as on a beach) and the larvae penetrate the skin. Yes, the larvae can penetrate through a beach blanket. Hookworms are typically susceptible to the same medications used to treat ascarids.

WHIPWORMS

Whipworms latch on to the lower aspects of the dog's colon and can cause cramping and diarrhea. Eggs do not start to appear in the dog's feces until about three months after the dog was infected. This worm has a peculiar life cycle, which makes it more difficult to control than ascarids or hookworms. The good thing is that whipworms rarely are transferred to people.

Some of the medications used to treat ascarids and hookworms are also effective against whipworms, but, in general, a separate treatment protocol is needed. Since most of the medications are effective against the adults but not the eggs or larvae, treatment is typically repeated in three weeks, and then often in three months as well. Unfortunately, since dogs don't develop resistance to whipworms, it is difficult to prevent them from getting reinfected if they visit soil contaminated with whipworm eggs.

TAPEWORMS

There are many different species of tapeworm that affect dogs, but *Dipylidium caninum* is probably the most common; it is spread by fleas. Flea larvae feed on organic debris and tapeworm eggs in the environment and, when a dog chews at himself and manages to ingest fleas, he might get a dose of tapeworm at the same time. The tapeworm then develops further in the intestine of the dog.

The tapeworm itself, which attaches to the intestinal wall, is composed of numerous segments. When the segments break off into the intestine (as proglottids), they may accumulate around the rectum, like grains of rice. While this tapeworm is disgusting in its behavior, it is not directly communicable to humans (although humans can also get infected by swallowing fleas).

A much more dangerous tapeworm is *Echinococcus multilocularis*, which is typically found in foxes, coyotes and

Adult whipworm, *Trichuris* sp., an intestinal parasite.

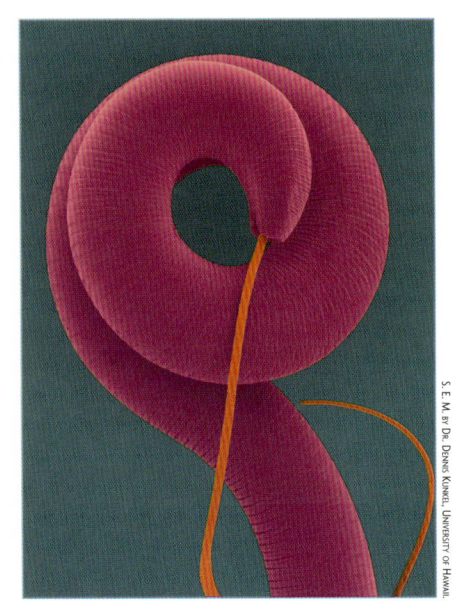

S.E.M. BY DR. DENNIS KUNKEL, UNIVERSITY OF HAWAII

Healthcare

wolves. The eggs are passed in the feces and infect rodents, and, when dogs eat the rodents, the dogs can be infected by thousands of adult tapeworms. While the parasites don't cause many problems in dogs, this is considered the most lethal worm infection that people can get. Take appropriate precautions if you live in an area in which these tapeworms are found. Do not use mulch that may contain feces of dogs, cats or wildlife, and discourage your pets from hunting wildlife. Treat these tapeworm infections aggressively in pets, because if humans get infected, approximately half die.

HEARTWORM

Heartworm disease is caused by the parasite *Dirofilaria immitis* and is seen in dogs around the world. The parasite itself, another of the nematodes, is spread between dogs by the bite of an infected mosquito. The mosquito injects infective larvae into the dog's skin with its bite, and these larvae develop under the skin for a period of time before making their way to the heart. There they develop into adults, which grow and create blockages of the heart, lungs and major blood vessels there. They also start producing offspring (microfilariae), and these microfilariae circulate in the bloodstream, waiting to hitch a ride when the next mosquito bites. Once in the mosquito, the microfilariae develop into infective larvae and the entire process is repeated.

When dogs get infected with heartworm, over time they tend to develop symptoms associated with heart disease, such as coughing, exercise intolerance and potentially many other manifestations. Diagnosis is confirmed by either seeing the microfilariae themselves in blood samples or using immunologic tests (antigen testing) to identify the presence of adult heartworms. Antigen testing is

A dog tapeworm proglottid (body segment).

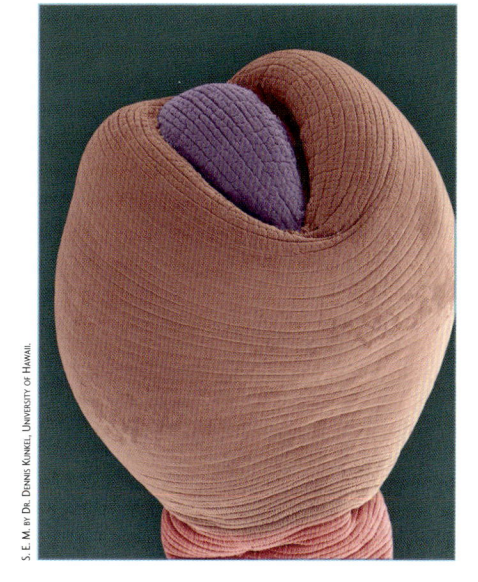

The dog tapeworm *Taenia pisiformis*.

A Look at Internal Parasites

Ascarid *Rhabditis*
(Photo by Carolina Biological Supply Co.)

Hookworm *Ancylostoma caninum*
(Photo by Carolina Biological Supply Co.)

Tapeworm *Dipylidium caninum*
(Photo by Tam C. Nguyen)

Heartworm *Dirofilaria immitis*
(Photo by Tam C. Nguyen)

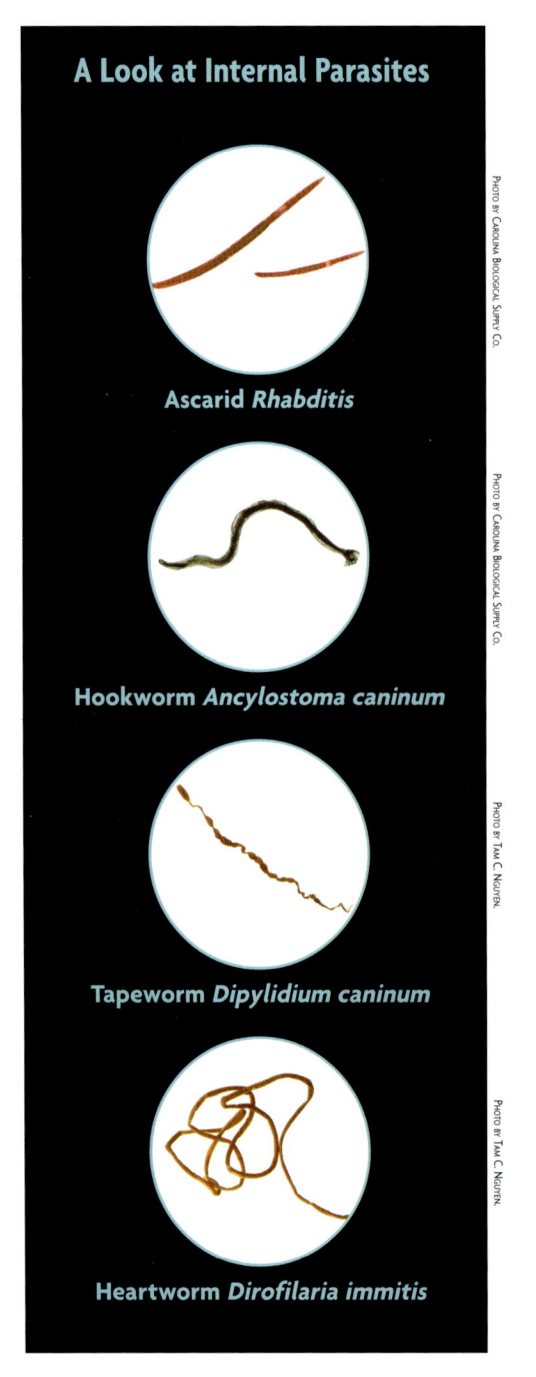

the most sensitive method of diagnosis, but it depends on the prevalence of infection in a given area. Since antigen tests measure the presence of adult heartworms, and microfilarial tests measure offspring produced by adults, neither are positive until six to seven months after the initial infection. However, the beginning of damage can occur by fifth-stage larvae as early as three months after infection. Thus it is possible for dogs to be harboring problem-causing larvae for up to three months before either type of test would identify an infection.

The good news is that there are great protocols available for preventing heartworm in dogs. Testing is critical in the process, and it is important to understand the benefits as well as the limitations of such testing. It is not necessary to test dogs younger than six months of age, because they have not yet had time for adults to develop and to produce microfilariae. All dogs six months of age or older that have not been on continuous heartworm preventive medication should be screened with microfilarial or antigen tests. For dogs receiving preventive medication, periodic antigen testing helps assess the effectiveness of the preventives as well as the owners' compliance in giving the medication. The American

Healthcare

Life Cycle of the Heartworm

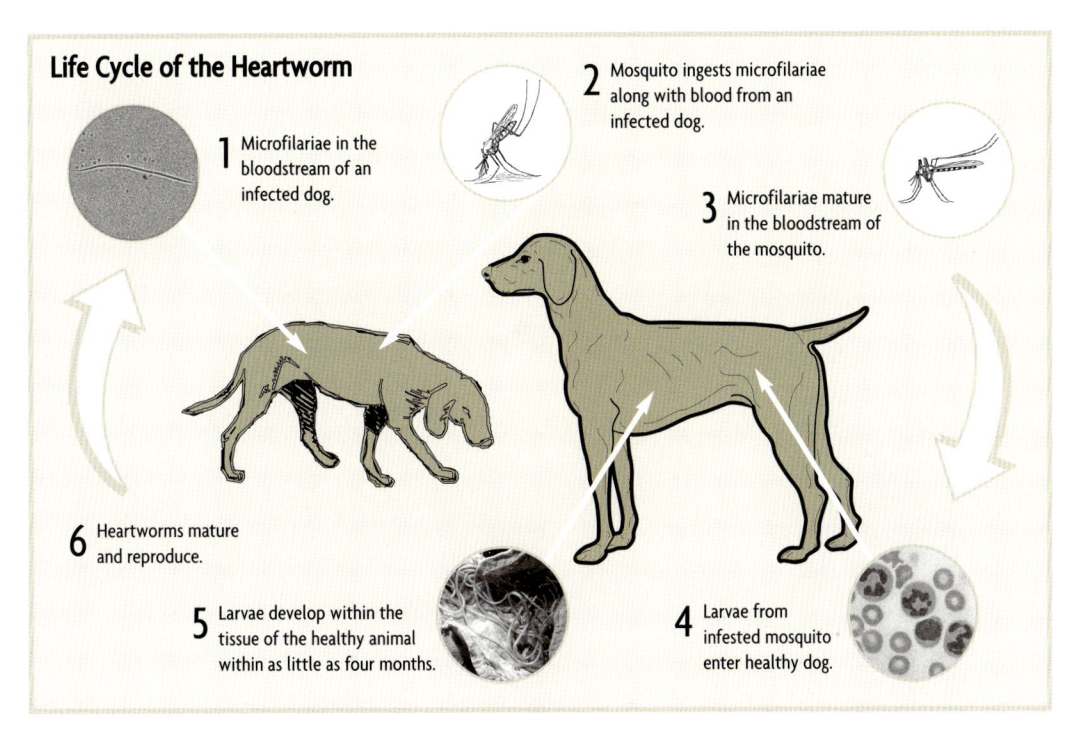

1. Microfilariae in the bloodstream of an infected dog.
2. Mosquito ingests microfilariae along with blood from an infected dog.
3. Microfilariae mature in the bloodstream of the mosquito.
4. Larvae from infested mosquito enter healthy dog.
5. Larvae develop within the tissue of the healthy animal within as little as four months.
6. Heartworms mature and reproduce.

Heartworm Society guidelines suggest that annual retesting may not be necessary when owners have absolutely provided continuous heartworm prevention. Retesting on a two- to three-year interval may be sufficient in these cases. However, your veterinarian will likely have specific guidelines under which heartworm preventives will be prescribed, and many prefer to err on the side of safety and retest annually.

It is indeed fortunate that heartworm is relatively easy to prevent, because treatments can be as life-threatening as the disease itself. Treatment requires a two-step process that kills the adult heartworms first and then the microfilariae. Dead circulating worms and microfilariae can lodge in a variety of tissues with adverse effects. Prevention is obviously preferable; this involves a once-monthly oral or topical treatment. Talk to your vet about your Komondor's sensitivity to parasite preventives as well as what other preventives he is on so that you do not risk overdosing with chemicals. Some heartworm preventives also offer protection against other internal parasites, fleas and some types of tick.

IMPORTANT HEALTH CONSIDERATIONS
By Joy C. Levy

ANESTHESIA SENSITIVITY
Be certain that your veterinarian realizes that Komondors are sensitive to anesthesia. In the old days, the author recalls, many Komondors were accidentally killed by vets attempting to anesthetize them for hip radiographs. The injections were administered on the basis of the dog's weight and the Komondor's coat can weigh 10 pounds or more, generally 10% of the dog's weight. Thankfully, vets today take precautions.

Before administering anesthesia, blood work is done to check for any problems, especially with the urinary or kidney functions. To correctly administer anesthesia is a skill, and different vets have different methods. If the Komondor is being prepared for a hip x-ray, gas anesthesia is not necessarily used; the Orthopedic Foundation for Animals advises using "chemical restraint to the point of muscle relaxation." Since radiography is not usually a painful procedure, unless the dog's hips are especially bad, gases are not used.

Generally gases like isoflurane and sevoflurane are chosen when the dog is having dental cleaning or a form of surgery. The dog's weight is not a factor when administering gas anesthesia. It is admistered to effect. There are quite a number of chemicals that are used by veterinarians for sedation: acepromazine and valium are two older ones. There are many newer ones. Whatever your vet is comfortable with is the one to go for. These sedatives or tranquilizers are administered on the basis of body weight. That is when it is vital to proceed with caution and start with an underdose. The more confident and relaxed the dog is, the more likely he is to go under with a very small dose. The dog who is uptight may require more. Local anesthesia is always preferred to general whenever a common radiograph is being performed.

It's up to responsible owners to make sure that your Komondor receives quality professional veterinary care. You are best to find a veterinarian whom you trust and to stay current on veterinary studies related to the breed.

HIP DYSPLASIA
Dogs 24 months of age and older should have their hips x-rayed; these x-rays are then submitted to the Orthopedic Foundation for Animals (OFA) for evaluation to determine if any degree of dysplasia is present. There are seven possible grades: Excellent, Good, Fair, Borderline, Mild, Moderate and Severe. Excellent, Good and Fair are considered

Do You Know about Hip Dysplasia?

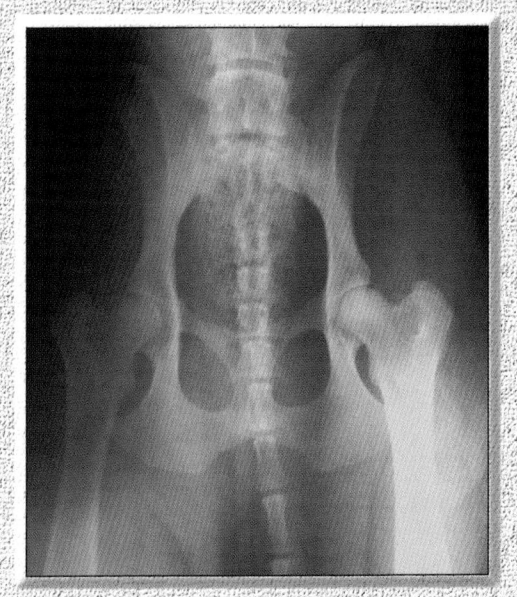

X-ray of a dog with "Good" hips.

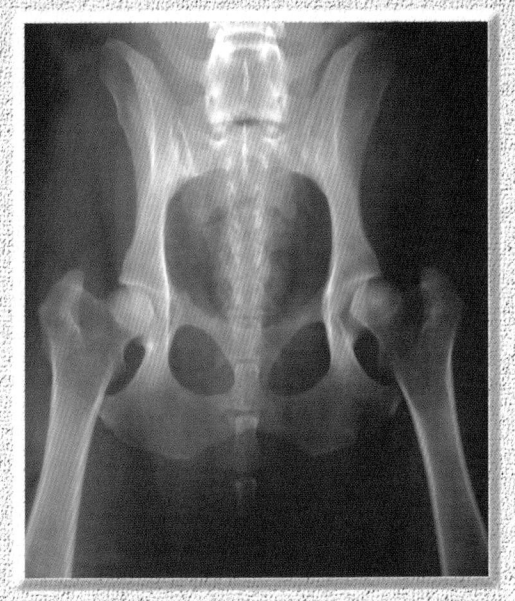

X-ray of a dog with "Moderate" dysplastic hips.

Hip dysplasia is a fairly common condition found in pure-bred dogs. When a dog has hip dysplasia, his hind leg has an incorrectly formed hip joint. By constant use of the hip joint, it becomes more and more loose, wears abnormally and may become arthritic.

Hip dysplasia can only be confirmed with an x-ray, but certain symptoms may indicate a problem. Your dog may have a hip dysplasia problem if he walks in a peculiar manner, hops instead of smoothly runs, uses his hind legs in unison (to keep the pressure off the weak joint), has trouble getting up from a prone position or always sits with both legs together on one side of his body.

As the dog matures, he may adapt well to life with a bad hip, but in a few years the arthritis develops and many dogs with hip dysplasia become crippled.

Hip dysplasia is considered an inherited disease and can be diagnosed definitively by x-ray only when the dog is two years old, although symptoms often appear earlier. Some experts claim that a special diet might help your puppy outgrow the bad hip, but the usual treatments are surgical. The removal of the pectineus muscle, the removal of the round part of the femur, reconstructing the pelvis and replacing the hip with an artificial one are all surgical interventions that are expensive, but they are usually very successful. Follow the advice of your veterinarian.

Your Komondor relies on you for proper care and good health. When properly maintained, he will remain a lively friend throughout his life.

normal and dogs with these gradings will receive an OFA number. The other four gradings do not warrant an OFA number, with the latter three indicating that the dog is affected by some level of dysplasia. Dogs that do not receive OFA numbers should not be used in breeding programs.

When visiting a litter, a potential owner should ask to see documentation of the litter's parents' hip clearances from the OFA or another accredited organization; similar hip-testing schemes are in place in countries around the world. Good breeders have all of their breeding stock tested and only breed from those dogs and bitches who have received appropriate clearances.

OTHER HEALTH CONCERNS

Diarrhea: Diarrhea is bad for any dog, but with a fully corded Komondor it is a disaster. The very first thing to check for is parasites. This might be overlooked, but in quite a few cases of persistent problems, the causes were parasites, usually whipworms, hookworms, *Giardia* or *Coccidiae*. Sometimes if a dog has a really severe bout of diarrhea, the feces is so diluted that nothing turns up in the first specimen. You may have to have more than one fecal test done. I think many of us forget to check the stool of grown dogs; dogs can pick up parasites at any time, especially if they are exercised in areas where other dogs also relieve themselves.

When a dog has a very severe bout of diarrhea, it can take a long time for his stomach to get back to normal. Do not be too quick to put him back on his usual diet. Several different manufacturers make "intestinal-diet" formulas, either prescription or available in pet-supply shops, which are a great help with this, but you must keep the dog on it for quite a while. These diets come in dry and canned form, and Komondors find that the dry form is much more palatable than the canned product. In case of severe diarrhea or any time you think your dog is dehydrated, recipes for an electrolyte solution and some bland diets you can make yourself are in the MASKC's *Komondor Cookbook.*

One Komondor owner reported bad effects his Komondor suffered from taking metronidazole for diarrhea. This is now the drug of choice with many veterinarians, and we and many others have used it with no bad side effects. Komondors (and probably other breeds as well) can react badly to either drugs or doses of drugs that most dogs tolerate well. You just have to be careful with any medication. After diarrhea and/or medication to control this, we give our dogs a tablespoon of yogurt daily to restore beneficent bacteria. Get a brand that has acidophilus cultures, or buy acidophilus capsules.

Bloat: Cases of bloat are reported in the Komondor every year. Most often it is an older dog, and some have died. However, there have been several cases of bloat in young dogs too. Bloat, also referred to as gastric torsion and gastric dilatation/volvulus, in the breed has been written about very frequently, but if one new reader can recognize the symptoms and thus save a dog, it is worth my taking the space here.

The first and most crucial thing to know is that in bloat cases, time is so important! A dog going into bloat is uncomfortable. He cannot lie down for any length of time, and he is restless. He may try to vomit or to defecate, and he may throw up small quantities of fluid and bile, but he cannot relieve the gas that is filling his stomach. Many dogs, even stoic Komondors, will whimper or cry out in pain. If you feel the stomach, it will be getting hard and tight.

This is an emergency situation. We cannot stress too strongly that every Komondor owner should know where to take his dog in an emergency. That means that you should find out where there is an emergency clinic that is open all night and on holidays and also be sure that you know how to get there before you need to. If your dog contracts bloat, he needs immediate attention, and it somehow always happens in the middle of the night or during a snowstorm, etc., so be proactive and be prepared!

Ask your vet for advice about bloat and where to take your dog for treatment. Some veterinary clinics are used to handling bloat cases; others are not. Have the emergency clinic's phone number in a place where you can find it quickly. If bloat occurs, call ahead and tell them you are on your

What Is "Bloat" and How Do I Prevent it?

You likely have heard the term "bloat," which refers to gastric torsion (gastric dilatation/volvulus), a potentially fatal condition. As it is directly related to feeding and exercise practices, a brief explanation here is warranted. The term *dilatation* means that the dog's stomach is filled with air, while *volvulus* means that the stomach is twisted around on itself, blocking the entrance/exit points. Dilatation/volvulus is truly a deadly combination, although they also can occur independently of each other. An affected dog cannot digest food or pass gas, and blood cannot flow to the stomach, causing accumulation of toxins and gas along with great pain and rapidly occuring shock.

Many theories exist on what exactly causes bloat, but we do know that deep-chested breeds are more prone. Activities like eating a large meal, gulping water, strenuous exercise too close to mealtimes or a combination of these factors can contribute to bloat, though not every case is directly related to these more well-known causes. With that in mind, we can focus on incorporating simple daily preventives and knowing how to recognize the symptoms. In addition to the tips presented in this book, ask your vet about how to prevent and recognize bloat. An affected dog needs immediate veterinary attention, as death can result quickly. Signs include obvious restlessness/discomfort, crying in pain, drooling/excessive salivation, unproductive attempts to vomit or relieve himself, visibly distended abdomen and collapsing. Do not wait: get to the vet *right away* if you see any of these symptoms. The vet will confirm by x-ray if the stomach is bloated with air; if so, the dog must be treated *immediately*.

As varied as the causes of bloat are the tips for prevention, but some common preventive methods follow:
- Feed two or three small meals daily rather than one large one;
- Do not feed water before, after or with meals, but allow access to water at all other times;
- Never permit rapid eating or gulping of water;
- No exercise for the dog at least two hours before and (especially) after meals;
- Feed high-quality food with adequate protein, adequate fiber content and not too much fat and carbohydrate;
- Explore herbal additives, enzymes or gas-reduction products (only under a vet's advice) to encourage a "friendly" environment in the dog's digestive system;
- Avoid foods and ingredients known to produce gas;
- Avoid stressful situations for the dog, especially at mealtimes;
- Make dietary changes gradually, over a period of a few weeks;
- Do not feed dry food only;
- Although the role of genetics as a causative of bloat is not known, many breeders do not breed from previously affected dogs;
- Sometimes owners are advised to have gastropexy (stomach stapling) performed on their dogs as a preventive measure;
- Pay attention to your dog's behavior and any changes that could be symptomatic of bloat. Your dog's life depends on it!

way. This will give your dog the best possible chance to survive. Untreated bloat is fatal, and it is a painful death.

Cysts: Komondors, especially older ones, get a lot of cysts. They are usually not malignant. Your veterinarian should advise you about them, of course, but the usual advice, when the vet is sure that they are not malignant, is to ignore them unless they are in a place where they get irritated constantly, are very unsightly or open on their own and do not heal. If they open on their own, it's best to have the vet check to see if he needs to clean them out; they often have a sac that should be removed. Mammary tumors are more often malignant, and these must be removed. Whether radiation after surgery is indicated is a matter between you and your vet. If your Komondor has to be anesthetized for some other reason, check the cysts beforehand, and perhaps your vet can remove them when he is doing the other procedure to minimize the amount of times that the dog needs to be anesthetized.

Skin Problems: The subject of skin problems is a very tricky one. Dogs whose parents have skin problems are likely to inherit a tendency to have them. Chewing hair off the legs also seems to be an inherited problem. Although generally hardy dogs, quite a few Komondors are allergic to something, and it is often very difficult to pinpoint the problem. Flea allergies are fairly common as well as allergies to inhaled pollen. If it turns out that the dog is allergic to pollen or other things in his environment, it is very hard to deal with. If testing has ruled out other allergens, and the allergen is something environmental that you cannot change (like pollen from trees in the area), your dog can get relief by taking Benadryl for the brief time that the offending allergen is in the air. More serious problems may warrant a prescription of steroids. If he is allergic to a product in your house (like the carpet, a household cleaner, etc.), you can change the product. If it is a food allergy, you can try to find a more suitable food. All too often, though, you can't find the culprit. Thankfully, young dogs who seem unable to keep a coat often simply get over the problem and end up without serious skin problems.

Another source of itching can be sarcoptic mange. It is sometimes hard to pick up mange mites in skin scrapings. In some cases an owner becomes affected by mange before the dog's problem is diagnosed. Fortunately anti-mange medications are well tolerated by both dogs and people!

SHOWING YOUR KOMONDOR

Judges Thelma Von Thaden, Lina Basquette and Tibor Brody with their Best in Show winner at the first World Komondor Show in Pennsylvania. The dog is Int. Ch. Argentina-Teri Felix, bred by Ferenc Lehoczky, with owner Andras Povazson.

Is dog showing in your blood? Are you excited by the idea of gaiting your handsome Komondor around the ring to the thunderous applause of an enthusiastic audience? Are you certain that your beloved Komondor is flawless? You are not alone! Every loving owner thinks that his dog has no faults, or too few to mention. No matter how many times an owner reads the breed standard, he cannot find any faults in his aristocratic companion dog. If this sounds like you, and if you are considering entering your Komondor in a dog show, here are some basic questions to ask yourself:

- Did you purchase a "show-quality" puppy from the breeder?
- Is your puppy at least six months of age?
- Does the puppy exhibit correct show type for his breed?
- Does your puppy have any disqualifying faults?
- Is your Komondor registered with the American Kennel Club?
- How much time do you have to devote to training, grooming, conditioning and exhibiting your dog?
- Do you understand the rules and regulations of a dog show?
- Do you have time to learn how to show your dog properly?
- Do you have the financial resources to invest in showing your dog?
- Will you show the dog yourself or hire a professional handler?
- Do you have a vehicle that can accommodate your weekend trips to the dog shows?

Success in the show ring requires more than a pretty face, a waggy tail and a pocketful of liver. Even though dog shows can be exciting and enjoyable, the sport of conformation makes great demands

FOR MORE INFORMATION...

For reliable, up-to-date information about registration, dog shows and other canine competitions, contact one of the national registries by mail or via the Internet.

American Kennel Club
5580 Centerview Dr., Raleigh, NC 27606-3390
www.akc.org

United Kennel Club
100 E. Kilgore Road, Kalamazoo, MI 49002
www.ukcdogs.com

Canadian Kennel Club
89 Skyway Ave., Suite 100, Etobicoke, Ontario M9W 6R4, Canada
www.ckc.ca

The Kennel Club
1-5 Clarges St., Piccadilly, London W1Y 8AB, UK
www.the-kennel-club.org.uk

showing and what's required to get started. Although the entry fee into a dog show is nominal, there are lots of other hidden costs involved with "finishing" your Komondor, that is, making him a champion. Things like equipment, travel, training and conditioning all cost money. A more serious campaign will include fees for a professional handler, boarding, cross-country travel and advertising. Top-winning show dogs can represent a very considerable investment—over $100,000 has been spent in campaigning some dogs. (The investment can be less, of course, for owners who don't use professional handlers.)

Many owners, on the other hand, enter their "average" Komondors in dog shows for the fun and enjoyment of it. Dog showing makes an absorbing hobby, with many rewards for dogs and owners alike. If you're having fun, meeting other people who

Each Komondor is gaited so that the judge can evaluate movement. Here is Bob Stebbins with Ch. Hercegvaros Enek.

on the exhibitors and the dogs. Winning exhibitors live for their dogs, devoting time and money to their dogs' presentation, conditioning and training. Very few novices, even those with good dogs, will find themselves in the winners' circle, though it does happen. Don't be disheartened, though. Every exhibitor began as a novice and worked his way up to the Group ring. It's the "working your way up" part that you must keep in mind.

Assuming that you have purchased a puppy of the correct type and quality for showing, let's begin to examine the world of

Here is a fairly uncommon sight: dozens of Komondors entered in a single show.

share your interests and enjoying the overall experience, you likely will catch the "bug." Once the dog-show bug bites, its effects can last a lifetime; it's certainly much better than a deer tick! Soon you will be envisioning yourself in the center ring at the Westminster Kennel Club Dog Show in New York City, competing for the prestigious Best in Show cup. This magical dog show is televised annually from Madison Square Garden, and the victorious dog becomes a celebrity overnight.

AKC CONFORMATION SHOWING

GETTING STARTED

Visiting a dog show as a spectator is a great place to start. Pick up the show catalog to find out what time your breed is being shown, who is judging the breed and in which ring the classes will be held. To start, Komondors compete against other Komondors, and the winner is selected as Best of Breed by the judge. This is the procedure for each breed. At a group show, all of the Best of Breed winners go on to compete for Group One (first place) in their respective groups. For example, all Best of Breed winners in a given group compete against each other; this is done for all seven groups. Finally, all seven group winners go head to head in the ring for the Best in Show award.

What most spectators don't understand is the basic idea of conformation. A dog show is often referred to as a "conformation" show. This means that the judge should decide how each dog stacks up (conforms) to the breed standard for his given breed: how well does this Komondor conform to the ideal representative detailed in the standard? Ideally, this is what happens. In reality, however, this ideal often gets slighted as the judge compares Komondor #1 to Komondor #2. Again, the ideal is that each dog is judged based on his merits in comparison to his breed standard, not in comparison to the other dogs in the ring. It is easier for judges to compare dogs of the same breed to decide which they think is the better specimen; in the Group and Best in Show rings, however, it is very difficult to compare one breed to another, like apples to oranges. Thus the dog's conformation to the breed standard—not to mention advertising dollars and good handling—is essential to success in conformation shows. The dog described in the standard (the standard for each AKC breed is written and approved by the breed's national parent club and then submitted to the AKC for approval) is the perfect dog of that breed, and breeders keep their eye on the standard when they choose which dogs to breed, hoping to get closer and closer to the ideal with each litter.

Another good first step for the novice is to join a dog club. You will be astonished by the many and different kinds of dog clubs in the country, with about 5,000 clubs holding events every year. Most clubs require that prospective new members present two letters of recommendation from existing members. Perhaps you've made some friends visiting a show held by a particular club and you would like to join that club. Dog clubs may specialize in a single breed, like a regional Komondor club, or in a specific pursuit, such as obedience trials or tracking. There are all-breed clubs for all dog enthusiasts; they sponsor special training days, seminars on topics like grooming or handling or lectures on breeding or canine genetics. There are also clubs that specialize in certain types of dogs, like livestock guard dogs, hunting dogs, companion dogs, etc.

> **MEET THE AKC**
> The American Kennel Club is the main governing body of the dog sport in the United States. Founded in 1884, the AKC consists of 500 or more independent dog clubs plus 4,500 affiliated clubs, all of which follow the AKC rules and regulations. Additionally, the AKC maintains a registry for pure-bred dogs in the US and works to preserve the integrity of the sport and its continuation in the country. Over 1,000,000 dogs are registered each year, representing over 150 recognized breeds. There are over 15,000 competitive events held annually for which over 2,000,000 dogs enter to participate. Dogs compete to earn over 40 different titles, from Champion to Companion Dog to Master Agility Champion.

148 KOMONDOR

Though rare in the US, benched shows are wonderful events for spectators and handlers alike. Visitors can meet the dogs in the benching area, where they stay when not competing, and learn more about the breed from the owners and breeders present.

Line 'em up. A herd of Koms at a club specialty in Burgdorf, Germany.

A parent club is the national organization, sanctioned by the AKC, which promotes and safeguards its breed in the country.

The Komondor Club of America was formed in 1967 and can be contacted on the Internet at http://clubs.akc.org/kca/. Another prominent club in the US is the Middle Atlantic States Komondor Club, www.maskc.org. Both clubs promote the Komondor and sponsor shows for the breed. The parent club holds an annual national specialty show, usually in a different city each year, in which many of the country's top dogs, handlers and breeders gather to compete. At a specialty show, only members of a single breed are invited to participate. There are also group specialties, in which all members of a group are invited. For more information about dog clubs in your area, contact the AKC at www.akc.org on the Internet or write them at their Raleigh, NC address.

How Shows Are Organized

Three kinds of conformation shows are offered by the AKC. There is the all-breed show, in which all AKC-recognized breeds can compete; the specialty show, which is for one breed only and usually sponsored by the breed's parent club; and the group show, for all breeds in one of the AKC's seven groups. The Komondor competes in the Working Group.

For a dog to become an AKC champion of record, the dog must earn 15 points at shows. The points must be awarded by at least three different judges and must include two "majors" under different judges. A "major" is a three-, four- or five-point win, and the number of points per win is determined by the number of dogs competing in the show on that day. (Dogs that are absent or are excused are not counted.) The number of points that are awarded varies from breed to breed. More dogs are needed to attain a major in more popular breeds, and fewer dogs are needed in less popular breeds. Yearly, the AKC evaluates the number of dogs in competition in each division (there are 14 divisions in all, based on geography) and may or may not change the numbers of dogs required for each number of points. For example, a major in Division 2 (Delaware, New Jersey and Pennsylvania) recently required four dogs or six bitches for a three-point major, eight dogs or eight bitches for a four-point major and nine dogs or ten bitches for a five-point major.

Only one dog and one bitch of each breed can win points at a given show. There are no "co-ed" classes except for champions of record. Dogs and bitches do not compete against each other until they are champions. Dogs that are not champions (referred to as "class dogs") compete in one of five classes. The class in which a dog is entered depends on age and previous show wins. First there is the Puppy Class (sometimes divided further into classes for 6- to 12-month-olds and 12- to 18-month-olds); next is the Novice Class (for dogs that have no points toward their championship and whose only first-place wins have come in the Puppy Class or the Novice Class, the latter class limited to three first places); then there is the American-bred Class (for dogs bred in the US); the Bred-by-Exhibitor Class (for dogs handled by their breeders or by immediate family members of their breeders); and the Open Class (for any non-champions). Any dog may enter the Open Class, regardless of age or win history, but to be competitive the dog should be older and have ring experience.

The judge at the show begins judging the male dogs in the Puppy Class(es) and proceeds through the other classes. The judge awards first through fourth place in each class. The first-place winners of each class then compete with one another in the Winners Class to

The judge will evaluate each dog individually, including a hands-on inspection of the dog's mouth, head and body.

KOMONDOR

Int. Ch. Jászkiséri Kócos Csupor has won several Bests in Show in Europe.

determine Winners Dog. The judge then starts over with the bitches, beginning with the Puppy Class(es) and proceeding up to the Winners Class to award Winners Bitch, just as he did with the dogs. A Reserve Winners Dog and Reserve Winners Bitch are also selected; they could be awarded the points in the case of a disqualification.

The Winners Dog and Winners Bitch are the two that are awarded the points for their breed. They then go on to compete with any champions of record (often called "specials") of their breed that are entered in the show. The champions may be dogs or bitches; in this class, all are shown together.

The judge reviews the Winners Dog and Winners Bitch along with all of the champions to select the Best of Breed winner. The Best of Winners is selected between the Winners Dog and Winners Bitch; if one of these two is selected Best of Breed as well, he or she is automatically determined Best of Winners. Lastly, the judge selects Best of Opposite Sex to the Best of Breed winner. The Best of Breed winner then goes on to the group competition.

At a group or all-breed show, the Best of Breed winners from each breed are divided into their respective groups to compete against one another for Group One through Group Four. Group One (first place) is awarded to the dog that best lives up to the ideal for his breed as described in the standard. A group judge, therefore, must have a thorough working knowledge of many breed standards. After placements have been made in each group, the seven Group One winners (from the Sporting Group, Working Group, Hound Group, etc.) compete against each other for the top honor, Best in Show.

There are different ways to find out about dog shows in your area. The American Kennel Club's monthly magazine, the *American Kennel Gazette* is accompanied by the *Events Calendar*; this magazine is available through subscription. You can also look on the AKC's and your parent club's websites for information and check the event listings in your local newspaper.

Your Komondor must be six months of age or older and registered with the AKC in order to be entered in AKC-sanctioned shows in which there are classes for the Komondor. Your Komondor also must not possess any disqualifying faults and must be sexually intact. The reason for the latter is simple: dog shows are the proving grounds to determine which dogs and bitches are worthy of being bred. If they cannot be bred, that defeats the purpose! If you have spayed or neutered your dog, however, there are many AKC events other than conformation, such as obedience trials, agility trials and the Canine Good Citizen® Program, in which you and your Komondor can participate.

OTHER TYPES OF COMPETITION
In addition to conformation shows, the AKC holds a variety of other competitive events. Obedience trials, agility trials and tracking trials are open to all breeds, while hunting tests, field trials, lure coursing, herding tests and trials, earthdog tests and coonhound events are limited to specific breeds or groups of breeds. The Junior Showmanship program is offered to aspiring young handlers and their dogs, and the Canine Good Citizen® Program is an all-around good-behavior test open to all dogs, pure-bred and mixed.

OBEDIENCE TRIALS
Mrs. Helen Whitehouse Walker, a Standard Poodle fancier, can be credited with introducing obedience trials to the United States. In the 1930s she designed a series of exercises based on those of the Associated Sheep, Police, Army Dog Society of Great Britain. These exercises were intended to evaluate the working relationship between dog and owner. Since those early days of the sport in the US, obedience trials have grown more and more popular, and now more than 2,000 trials each year attract over 100,000 dogs and their owners. Any dog registered with the AKC, regardless of neutering or other disqualifications that would

A Komondor flying over the high jump at an obedience trial. Quite a sight!

> **JUNIOR SHOWMANSHIP**
> For budding dog handlers, ages 10 to 18 years, Junior Showmanship competitions are an excellent training ground for the next generation of dog professionals. Owning and caring for a dog are wonderful methods of teaching children responsibility, and Junior Showmanship builds upon that foundation. Juniors learn by grooming, handling and training their dogs, and the quality of a junior's presentation of the dog (and himself) is evaluated by a licensed judge. The junior can enter with any registered AKC dog to compete, including an Indefinite Listing Privilege, provided that the dog lives with him or a member of his family.
>
> Junior Showmanship competitions are divided into two classes: Novice (for beginners) and Open (for juniors who have three first place wins in the Novice Class). The junior must run with the dog with the rest of the handlers and dogs, stack the dog for examination and individually gait the dog in a specific pattern. Juniors should practice with a handling class or an experienced handler before entering the Novice Class so that they recognize all the jargon that the judge may use.
>
> A National Junior Organization was founded in 1997 to help promote the sport of dog showing among young people. The AKC also offers a Junior Scholarship for juniors who excel in the program.

preclude entry in conformation competition, can participate in obedience trials.

There are three levels of difficulty in obedience competition. The first (and easiest) level is the Novice, in which dogs can earn the Companion Dog (CD) title. The intermediate level is the Open level, in which the Companion Dog Excellent (CDX) title is awarded. The advanced level is the Utility level, in which dogs compete for the Utility Dog (UD) title. Classes at each level are further divided into "A" and "B," with "A" for beginners and "B" for those with more experience. In order to win a title at a given level, a dog must earn three "legs." A "leg" is accomplished when a dog scores 170 or higher (200 is a perfect score). The scoring system gets a little trickier when you understand that a dog must score more than 50% of the points available for each exercise in order to actually earn the points. Available points for each exercise range between 20 and 40. The first Komondor CD was Jacques Levy's Gyali Bicskas, and the first UD in the breed was Ch. Mount Everest Jancsi Jago, owned by Dr. Arthur Sorkin.

A dog must complete different exercises at each level of obedience. The Novice exercises are the easiest, with the Open and finally the Utility levels progressing in difficulty. Examples of Novice exercises are on- and off-lead heeling, a figure-8 pattern,

Showing

performing a recall (or come), long sit and long down and standing for examination. In the Open level, the Novice-level exercises are required again, but this time without a leash and for longer durations. In addition, the dog must clear a broad jump, retrieve over a jump and drop on recall. In the Utility level, the exercises are quite difficult, including executing basic commands based on hand signals, following a complex heeling pattern, locating articles based on scent discrimination and completing jumps at the handler's direction.

Once he's earned the UD title, a dog can go on to win the prestigious title of Utility Dog Excellent (UDX) by winning "legs" in ten shows. Additionally, Utility Dogs who win "legs" in Open B and Utility B earn points toward the lofty title of Obedience Trial Champion (OTCh.). Established in 1977 by the AKC, this title requires a dog to earn 100 points as well as three first places in a combination of Open B and Utility B classes under three different judges. The "brass ring" of obedience competition is the AKC's National Obedience Invitational. This is an exclusive competition for only the cream of the obedience crop. In order to qualify for the invitational, a dog must be ranked in either the top 25 all-breeds in obedience or in the top three for his breed in obedience. The title at stake here is that of National Obedience Champion (NOC).

AGILITY TRIALS

Agility trials became sanctioned by the AKC in August 1994, when the first licensed agility trials were held. Since that time, agility certainly has grown in popularity by leaps and bounds, literally! The AKC allows all registered breeds (including Miscellaneous Class breeds) to participate, providing the dog is 12 months of age or older. The Komondor has the

Begin showing your Komondor at a young age so that he will accept the show procedure as a normal event.

The first group winner in the breed in Holland, this Hungarian-bred Komondor went on to take Best in Show at a show in Amsterdam.

potential to excel in agility, but as yet few have performed in this venue.

Agility is designed so that the handler demonstrates how well the dog can work at his side. The handler directs his dog through, over, under and around an obstacle course that includes jumps, tires, the dog walk, weave poles, pipe tunnels, collapsed tunnels and more. While working his way through the course, the dog must keep one eye and ear on the handler and the rest of his body on the course. The handler runs along with the dog, giving verbal and hand signals to guide the dog through the course.

The first organization to promote agility trials in the US was the United States Dog Agility Association, Inc. (USDAA). Established in 1986, the USDAA sparked the formation of many member clubs around the country. To participate in USDAA trials, dogs must be at least 18 months of age.

The USDAA and AKC both offer titles to winning dogs, although the exercises and requirements of the two organizations differ. Agility Dog (AD), Advanced Agility Dog (AAD) and Master Agility Dog (MAD) are the titles offered by the USDAA, while the AKC offers Novice Agility (NA), Open Agility (OA), Agility Excellent (AX) and Master Agility Excellent (MX). Beyond these four AKC titles, dogs can win additional titles in "jumper" classes: Jumper with Weave Novice (NAJ), Open (OAJ) and Excellent (MXJ). The ultimate title in AKC agility is MACH, Master Agility Champion. Dogs can continue to add number designations to the MACH title, indicating how many times the dog has met the title's requirements (MACH1, MACH2 and so on).

TRACKING

Tracking tests are exciting ways to test your Komondor's instinctive scenting ability on a competitive level. All dogs have a nose, and all breeds are welcome in tracking tests, although the Komondor has not participated in tracking in great numbers. The breed does have an excellent nose, though, and could reach high levels of success in tracking.

The first AKC-licensed tracking test took place in 1937 as part of the Utility level at an obedience trial, and thus competitive tracking was officially begun. The first title, Tracking Dog (TD), was offered in 1947, ten years after the first official tracking test. It was not until 1980 that the AKC added the title Tracking Dog Excellent (TDX), which was followed by the title Variable Surface Tracking (VST) in 1995.

Champion Tracker (CT) is awarded to a dog who has earned all three of those titles.

The TD level is the first and most basic level in tracking, progressing in difficulty to the TDX and then the VST. A dog must follow a track laid by a human 30 to 120 minutes prior in order to earn the TD title. The track is about 500 yards long and contains up to 5 directional changes. At the next level, the TDX, the dog must follow a 3- to 5-hour-old track over a course that is up to 1,000 yards long and has up to 7 directional changes. In the most difficult level, the VST, the track is up to 5 hours old and located in an urban setting.

An impressive family: five titled members of the Hercegvaros E-litter with parents: the dam, Ch. Sarokhazi Cukor UD, and the sire, Ch. Szentivani Ingo.

INDEX

*Page numbers in **boldface** indicate illustrations.*

Abonyi 16, 36
Acidophilus 141
Activities 106
Activity level 73, 75
Adams, Buster and Henny 14, 20, 23, 111
Adenovirus 121
Adolescence 108
Adult
—adoption 90
—feeding 70
—health 117
—training 89-90
Agar 8
Aggression 25, 34, 62, 67, 91, 110, 115
Agility trials and titles 151, 153-154
All-breed show 150
Allergies 117, 143
American Heartworm Society 136
American Kennel Club 8, 144-145, 147-148, 150
—breed standard 16, 36
—competitive events 151-155
—conformation showing 146-151
—registrations 16
American Kennel Gazette 150
American-bred Class 149
Amitraz 128
Anal glands 85
Anatolian Shepherd Dog 10, 22
Ancylostoma caninum 133, 136
Anecdotes from owners 25
Anemia 71
Anesthesia sensitivity 118, 138, 143
Anghi Dr. Csaba 16, 36
Angyal's Espuela Magyar 15, 21, 22, 111
Annual vet exams 117
Antifreeze 57
Antigen testing 135
Appetite loss 123
Arch, Ann 11
Argentina-Teri Felix 144
Ascarid 132-133, 136
Ascaris lumbricoides 132
Astiagis, King 12
Attention 98-99, 104
Babesiosis 126
Barking 28, 110
Bathing 76, 80-82
Bedding 53, 59, 93
Begging 70
Beregi, Oscar 12-14
Bergamasco 10
Best in Show 146-147, 150
—first win 13
Best of Breed 146, 150
Best of Opposite Sex 150
Best of Winners 150
Biting out of fear 108
Bloat 69-70, 71, 73-74, 75, 141-143
Blumenthal, Dr. J.C. 82
Boarding 87
Body language 91, 95, 102
Bones 54
Booster shots 123
Bordetella 121-122
Borrelia burgdorferi 121, 129
Borsodi Gango 48
Bowls 51
Boytar-Da-Co-Tah Abba 36
Boytar-Da-Co-Tah Atok 23
Boytar-Hercegvaros Balna 17
Boytar-Hercegvaros Bocs 16
Bred-by-Exhibitor Class 149
Breeders 35, 140, 147
—selection 46, 49, 113

Breeding of 32-35, 49
Bukovski, Joszef 45
Canada 12, 15, 21
Canadian Kennel Club 145
Cancer 123
Canine cough 121
Canine Good Citizen® 106, 151
Car travel 86
Cats 30
Champion 148
Champion Tracker 155
Chasing animals 109
Chew toys 53, 64, 93-94
—guarding 30
Chewing 53, 63
Cheyletiella mites 130
Cheyletiellosis 130
Chiggers 131
Children 30, 58, 60, 63, 65, 91
Chocolate 70
Choke collar 31, 55, 99
Classes at shows 149
Clicker training 108
Clippers 80
Clubs 147
Coat 13, 16, 77
—care 75-82
—color 34
Coccidiae 140
Cognitive dysfunction 117
Collar 31, 55, 98
Come 103, 109
Comenius, Amos 12
Commands 64, 67, 97, 100-106, 109
Commitment of ownership 49-50
Companion dog 23-24, 28, 32
Companion Dog Excellent 152
Companion Dog title 152
Competitive events 151-155
Conformation shows 146
—classes at 149
—getting started 146
—requirements for 150
Consistency 61, 64, 94, 100
Coppinger, Raymond 14
Corded breeds 10, 13, 17
Corded coat 13, 16, 19, 22, 75-78, 81
—requirement in breed standard 16
Coronavirus 121-122
Correction 98, 109, 111
Counter surfing 67
Courage 51
Crate 51, 58-59, 66, 77, 80, 93
—pads 53
—training 50, 92-94, 96
Crying 59, 66, 93
Ctenocephalides canis 124
Cutaneous larval migrans 133
Cysts 117, 143
Dangers in the home 56-57
Danoff, Saul 26
Davis, Ann 11
De Cholnoky, Dr. Tibor 12
Deer tick 129
DEET 129
Demodex mites 131
Demodicosis 131
Dental care 84, 115, 117, 123
Development 69, 72
Diarrhea 73, 140
Diary of Maggie, The 20, 111
Diet 67-74, 140, 142-143
Dilatation 69-70, 71, 73-74, 75, 141-143
Diosgyori Herceg Kajla 26-27
Dipylidium caninum 134, 136

Dirofilaria immitis 135, 136
Discipline 62, 96-97
Distemper 121-122
Dogs 15
Dogs of Hungary, The 20
Down 65, 95, 100, 102, 109
Down/stay 103
Drying 81
Duna 13, 16, 18, 22-23, 26-27, 29, 37, 39, 48, 155
Ear
—cleaning 82
—mite infestation 131
—removing hair from 79, 82
Echinococcus multilocularis 134
Ehrlichiosis 126, 129
Emergency care 141
England 11, 145
Erythema migrans 129
Evans, Dixie 12
Events Calendar 150
Evers, Irene 9, 18, 20, 26
Excessive thirst 72
Exercise 71, 74
—precautions 69, 75, 142
—schedule 75
Expenses of ownership 51
External parasites 124-131
Eye care 83
Family meeting the puppy 57
Fear 62
—biting 108
—period 61
Fecal test 140
Fédération Cynologique Internationale 36
—breed standard 42
Feeding 67-74, 93, 140-143
—adult 70
—puppy 35
—schedule 70, 72, 75
—senior dog 71
—special considerations 72, 142
Fenced yard 32, 57
First night in new home 58
Flea 124, 125, 126
—allergies 143
—control of 125
—preventives, sensitivity to 118, 125, 129, 137
Food 35, 67-74, 93, 142
—allergies 143
—bowls 51
—for stomach upset 140
—guarding 30, 67
—loss of interest in 123
—poisonous to dogs 70, 71
—rewards 67, 90, 106, 108
Fouti Hercules Jancsika 14
Fussy eater 73
Gabor, Zsa Zsa 14
Garlic 70
Gastric dilatation/volvulus 69-70, 71, 73-74, 75, 141-143
Gastric torsion 69-70, 71, 73-74, 75, 141-143
Gastropexy 142
Genetic testing 113
Giardia 121-122, 140
Goats 111
Grapes 70
Great Pyrenees 10, 15, 22
Gribbie, Mrs. 111
Grooming 75-85
Group competition 146-147
Guard dog 17, 23-25, 29, 32, 34, 107, 110
Guarding food/toys 30, 67

Gum disease 115
Gyali Bicskas 152
Halasi-Kun, Dr. George 36
Halmi, Robert 21
Halti collars 55
Hampshire College's Livestock Dog Project 14
Handler 144
Handling improperly 31
Hattyu 13
Head collars 55
Health 57
—adult 117
—considerations 118, 138
—insurance for pets 120
—journal 57
—puppy 46, 113
—senior dog 117
Heart disease 117
Heartworm 115, 135, 136, 137
Heartworm preventives 136
—sensitivity to 118, 125, 129, 137
Heat-related problems 86
Heel 104-106
Hepatitis 121-122
Hercegvaros Cica of Borvaale and Loakespark 11, 14
Hercegvaros Csupor at Borvaale 12
Hercegvaros E-litter 155
Hercegvaros Enek 145
Hercegvaros Ergike 25
Hercegvaros kennel 46
Hereditary concerns 47
Heterodoxus spiniger 130
Himalayas 11
Hip dysplasia 47, 138-140
Homemade toys 55
Hookworms 133, 136, 140
House-training 50-52, 73, 92-99
Hunor 18
Hungarian Dog Breeds 20
Hungarian Kennel Club 12, 36
Hungary 8, 12, 21, 23
—breed standard of 36
Hunor 18
Hunting tests 151
Identification 85-87
Imre, Ócsag 20
Incredible Dog, An: The Komondor and the Other Hungarian Shepherd Dogs 20
Independent thinker 25
Indian Run Acel Ropi 15
Indian Run Az Aranyos Chimera 21
Infectious diseases 120
Insect development inhibitors 125
Insect growth regulators 125
Insurance 120
Internal parasites 132
Ixodes dammini 127, 128
Ixodes pacificus 129
Ixodes scapularis 129
Jancsika 14
Jászkiséri Kócos Csupor 41, 150
Javictreva Camaraderie 34
Jeritza, Maria 14
Judges 149
Juliska 14
Jumper agility titles 154
Jumping up 64, 95
Junior Showmanship 151-152
Kakonyi, Peter 12
Karika 73
Katsányi, Dr. Zsigmond 11, 23
Kenéz, Zoltán 11, 20
Kennel Club, The 145

Kennel cough 122
Kennel dog 28
Kidney problems 117
Kincel, John and Carol 14
Kincs 73
Kiraly **9**
Kitten **14**
Komondor Club of America 13, 14, 21, 46
Komondor Cookbook 141
Komondor Defined, The 11
Kopo 8
Kuvasz 8, **10**, 22
Kurcafuredi-Subas Edi **17, 38**
Lajosmegyi Dahu Digal **20**
Lanz, Pat 11
Leash 29, 55, 98-99
—pulling on 105
—training 109
Leptospirosis 121
Levy, Jacques 152
Levy, Marion and Joy 13, 16, 18-19
Lifespan 71, 117
Livestock guard dog 10, 15, 17, 30, 107-111
—feeding 73
—in US 20, 22
—temperament 10, 22
Louse **130**
Lyme disease 121, 126, 128-129
—vaccine 122
Maggie 14, 22, 111
Magyar Kutyák, A **21**, 36
Magyars 9
Majors 149
Male 29
Mammary tumors 143
Mange 117, 130, 143
Maremma Sheepdog **10**, 22
Marking territory 111
Martingale collars 55
Master Agility Champion 154
Mat splitter 76, 78
McLellan, Mrs. R. D. 12
Medication 118
Metronidazole 141
Microchip 86
Microfilariae 135
Middle Atlantic States Komondor Club (MASKC) 13, 14, 20, 35, 46
Miscellaneous Class 153
Mites **128**, 130, **131**
Mosquitoes 129
Mount Everest Bitang 26
Mount Everest Jancsi Jago 152
Mount Everest kennel 18
Mouthing 31
Mudi 8
Mueller 16, 36
Nail clipping 79
Name 46, 99, 104
National Obedience Champion 153
Natural History 12
Negative reinforcement 109
Neighbors 111
Neutering 115, 123, 151
Nipping 63, 65
No 109
Novice Class 149
Nuts 70
Obedience 102
—instructor 106
—training 109
—trials 107, 151
Obedience Trial Champion 153
Obesity 70-71, 75
Off 65, 67, 95
Oh-M 26-27
Ohegyi Abrand Duna at Borvaale **11**
Ohegyi Aldar **40**

Okay 101, 105
Onions 70, 71
Open Class 149
Origin of breed 9
Orthopedic Foundation for Animals 47, 139-140
Orthopedic problems 15, 47, 74, 138-140
Other pets 28, 30, 91
Otodectes cynotis 131
Our National Treasure: The Hungarian Komondor 9, 18, 20
Outdoor safety 32, 57
Ownership 49-50
—expenses of 51
—suitability 31
Pack animals 61, 96-98
Paper-training 92
Parainfluenza 121
Parasite preventives
—sensitivity to 118, 125, 129, 137
Parasites 78
—external 124-131
—internal 132-137
Parent club 148, 150
Parvovirus 121-122
Patience 91
Personality 22-32
Pethe, Ferenc 12
Physical traits 48
Playtime 103
Poisons 56-57, 70-71
Police work 17
Pollen allergies 143
Positive reinforcement 58, 97, 100, 109
Possessive behavior 30, 67
Praise 90, 97, 106, 109
Predator control 107
Preventive care 113, 117-118
Prong collars 55
Protective nature 17, 23-25, 29, 32, 34, 107, 110
Puli 8, **10**, 13, 17
Pumi 8
Punishment 66, 96-98, 111
Puppy
—coat 76
—common problems 63
—establishing leadership 89, 108
—exercise 69, 75
—feeding 35, 68, 72
—first night in new home 58
—health 46, 113
—introducing to other animals 108
—kindergarten training class 99
—meeting the family 57
—personality 49, 115
—selection 46, 47, 49, 90, 113
—show quality 144-145
—socialization 59
—teething 64, 72
—training 62, 89
Puppy Class 149
Puppy-proofing 56
Puszta **18**
Rabies 121-122
Racka 9
Racz-Caroff, Anna 20
Rain 9
Raisins 70
Raitsis, Dr. Emil 11, 36
Rawhides 54
Red mange 131
Registration
—of working dogs 15
—numbers 16
—numbers in US 17
Related breeds 10
Reprimand 98, 109, 111

Requirements for show 150
Reserve Winners Bitch 150
Reserve Winners Dog 150
Respiratory disease 122
Retractable leads 56
Rewards 67, 90, 96, 97, 106
—food 97, 108
Rhabditis **136**
Rocky Mountain spotted fever 126
Rope toys 54
Roundworm **132**
Routine 94
Safety 51, 56, 71, 93, 94, 103, 142
—in the car 86
—outdoors 32, 57
—with children 30
—with toys 53-55
Sarcoptes scabiei **128**
Sarcoptes mites 130
Sarcoptic mange 117, 130, 143
Sárkány, Pál 20
Sarokhazi Cukor **155**
Scabies 130
Scent attraction 95
Schedule 68, 93-94
—exercise 75
—feeding 72, 75
Scissors 76-78
Seam rippers 76, 78
Seattle Kennel Club Dog Show 20
Senior dog 117
—diet 71
Sensitivity
—to anesthesia 118
—to medications 118
—to parasite preventives 118, 125, 129, 137
Sex differences 29, 48
Show-quality 144, 145
Shyness 108
Sit 100, 109
Sit/stay 102
Size 48
Skin problems 117, 143
Socialization 28, 59-62, 99, 115
Soft toys 54
Sorkin, Dr. Arthur 152
South Russian Ovcharka **10**, 11
Spaying 115, 123, 151
Specials 150
Specialty show 148
Squeaky toy 54
Standard 146
—American Kennel Club 16, 36
—FCI 42
—first 111
Stay 102, 105-106, 109
Sticks 54
Stomach stapling 142
Strangers 24, 30, 108, 110
Stuffed toys 54
Sudduth, Mrs. William H., III 12
Sunshine 11
Supervision 63-64, 94
Supplementation 69
Szentivani Ingo 13, 16, 18, **19**, 22-23, 26-27, 29, **37, 39, 48, 155**
Szentivani kennel 18, 46
Taenia pisiformis **135**
Tapeworms **134**, **135**, **136**
Tattoo 87
Teeth 84, 115, 117, 123
Teething 64, 72
Temperament 10, 22, 32, 46, 48, 118
—as family dog 28
—evaluation 115
Temperature, taking your dog's 115
Territory marking 111
Therapy dog 106

Thirst 72
Tibetan Mastiff 10, 22
Ticks 126, **127**, **128**, 129
Timing 95, 104
Toxins 56-57, 70-71
Toxocara canis **132**
Toys 53, 64, 93-94
Tracking 106, 151, 154
Traffic leads 56
Trainer 108
Training 29, 67
—basic principles 89
—commands 100, 106, 109
—consistency in 61, 64, 100
—crate 50, 92-94, 96
—early 62
—importance of timing 95, 104
—methods for livestock guards 108
—problems 31
—tips 63, 107-111
—toilet 92-99
Travel 51, 86
Treats 58, 67, 70, 90
—in training 97, 106, 108
Trentvaros A. Koda **18**
Trichuris sp. **134**
Tricks 106
Tumors 143
Tunney, Gene 14
Type 144-145
Un Chien Incroyable: le Komondor et les autres bergers Hongroise 20
United Kennel Club 145
United States 12-20
United States Deparment of Agriculture 15
United States Dog Agility Association 154
Utility Dog 152
Utility Dog Excellent 153
Vaccinations 57, 61, 115, 120-123
Varhegy Hunor **26**
Variable Surface Tracking 155
Veterinarian 22, 54, 57, 115, 117, 118-120, 125
Veterinary insurance 120
Videos 21
Visiting the litter 47, 49
Viszla 8
Volvulus 69-70, 71, 73-74, 75, 141-143
Walker, Mrs. Helen Whitehouse 151
Walking dandruff 130
Water 73, 142
—bowls 51, 93
—increased intake 72
Weaning 34, 68
Weather 9, 111
West Nile virus 129
Westminster Kennel Club 146
Whelping 32-35
Whining 59, 66, 93
Whipworms **134**, 140
White color 34
Winners Bitch 150
Winners Class 149
Winners Dog 150
With other pets 28, 30
With strangers 24, 30
Working dog 17, 24-25
Working Group 17
—first win 13
World War II 12
Worming medications
—sensitivity to 118, 125, 129, 137
X-rays 140
Yard 32, 57
—safety in 32
Yogurt 141
Zankowich, Maria 36
Zobraki Highland Spirit **12**

My Komondor

PUT YOUR PUPPY'S FIRST PICTURE HERE

Dog's Name _____

Date _____ Photographer _____